Psychology in Practice: Health

PSYCHOLOGY
in Practice

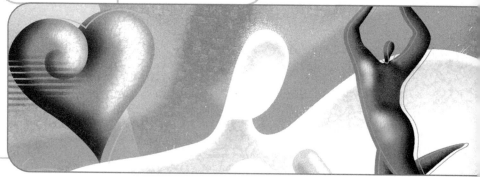

Health

Philip Banyard

Series Editor: Hugh Coolican

Hodder & Stoughton
A MEMBER OF THE HODDER HEADLINE GROUP

ACKNOWLEDGEMENTS

The author and publisher would like to thank the following for permission to reproduce material in this book:
Figure 5.1 Mullen and Johnson, (1990) The Psychology of Consumer Behaviour, Lawrence Earlbaum; Figure 5.4 Roger Ressmeyer, Starlight/Science Photo Library; Figure 6.1 Wellcome Library, London; Figure 6.2 Professor Blinkhorn, Health Education Journal; Figure 7.2 Fetal Alcohol and Drug Unit, University of Washington; Figure 8.1 Tek Image/Science Photo Library; Figure 8.3 Dowse and Ehlers, Global Ergonomics, Oxford: Elsevier.

Every effort has been made to obtain necessary permission with reference to copyright material. The publishers apologise if inadvertently any sources remain unacknowledged and will be glad to make the necessary arrangements at the earliest opportunity.

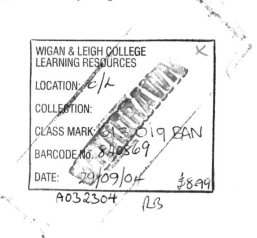
Orders: please contact Bookpoint Ltd, 130 Milton Park, Abingdon, Oxon OX14 4SB. Telephone: (44) 01235 827720. Fax: (44) 01235 400454. Lines are open from 9.00 – 6.00, Monday to Saturday, with a 24 hour message answering service.

British Library Cataloguing in Publication Data
A catalogue record for this title is available from the British Library

ISBN 0 340 84496 5

First Published 2002
Impression number   10 9 8 7 6 5 4
Year   2007 2006 2005 2004 2003

Typeset by Dorchester Typesetting Group Limited, Dorset, England.
Printed in Great Britain for Hodder & Stoughton Educational, a division of Hodder Headline, 338 Euston Road, London NW1 3BH by CPI Bath

CONTENTS

Preface

The aim of this text is give you an introduction into the wide range of links that have been made between psychology and the study of health and healthcare. I hope that the book provides a framework for study that enables you to go and study the subject in more detail, and I hope it is written in an interesting enough way to encourage you to do this. It is aimed, in particular, at students taking the OCR course in A Level psychology, but other people interested in the issues of health and psychology should also find much to engage them. To read this book, you do not need to have a detailed knowledge of psychology, though it would be helpful if you are aware of the basic concepts.

The book is divided up into eight chapters that deal with the current concerns of health psychology. These concerns have developed from the problems of health and healthcare, rather than from the research areas of psychology. The traditional approach to psychology has divided the subject into specialist areas such as cognitive psychology and physiological psychology. The approach in health psychology, on the other hand, is to use whatever psychology is useful. This means that evidence is often used from a wide range of psychological approaches when dealing with a health problem.

This book developed out of a series of lectures at the Nottingham Trent University. These lectures were designed to give students a broad overview of the field and encourage individual reading and individual research. In keeping with this approach, I have tried to provide a number of references in this book that will be useful for further reading and research. I have not, however, provided a long list of the various studies that support different positions in health psychology. I hope that readers will be able to go from this text to the more specialised works that are referred to, and also to the primary research if they are interested in a particular question. I have also tried, wherever possible, to concentrate on evidence and public policies from the United Kingdom, because our health service is unique and some aspects of our health psychology are, therefore, also unique.

It is a tradition in psychology texts to write in a dispassionate voice, as if the author does not have a personal bias. I have always been uncomfortable with this tradition, and I think it is not possible to write a book about human affairs without showing your bias. It is my belief that a society should protect and care for its citizens and should aim to offer universal healthcare for people regardless of their financial circumstances, class, gender or race. This value guides the way I view psychology and health.

Finally, this book is meant to be relatively easy to read while still covering a wide range of important issues. I hope that you enjoy reading it.

Acknowledgements

I would like to acknowledge the colleagues and friends who have read and commented on various parts of the text, and provided useful information. In particular, I would like to thank Lesley Phair, Patrick Hylton, Jeniba Grant, The Gladstone darts team and all my students whose ideas I have unwittingly or purposefully pinched.

Philip Banyard
Nottingham, October 2001

Introduction

In this introduction we will look at the ways we try to define good health, and the models of health that try to combine medical and psychological ideas. We will also look briefly at the development of healthcare in this country and the starting points for health psychology. Finally we will glance at the issue of social diversity and health.

What do we mean by good health?

When we are in good health we take it for granted, and when we get sick we curse our bad luck and look around for people or things to blame for our misfortune. But is our sickness a result of bad luck, or do we contribute to our own misfortune? The horrible truth is that we can reduce the probability of ill health by following some simple behavioural rules. A ten-year study of 7000 people (Breslow and Enstrom, 1980) found that on average people live longer and enjoy better health if they:

- sleep 7–8 hours a day
- have breakfast every day
- don't smoke
- rarely eat between meals
- are near to their prescribed weight
- drink no or just a small amount of alcohol
- take regular exercise.

In fact the study went as far as to say that people over the age of 75 who had followed these rules had an equal level of health to a 40-year-old who followed fewer than three of the rules.

Behaviour is related to health and illness, and psychology tries to investigate that behaviour, find the connections between behaviour and illness, and encourage people to behave in ways that protect their health. Sadly it looks as if I need to change my beer, lard and television lifestyle if I want to improve my chances of a long life. Before we look at how this can be achieved we need to take a step back and consider what we mean by health in the first place.

WHAT IS HEALTH?

The first question we have to look at is: what do we mean by health? This is by no means as straightforward as it sounds. Before reading on, try this exercise.

• **Table 0.1:** The distinction between health and illness

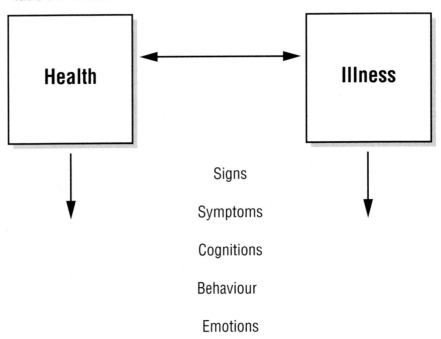

Our personal sense of being healthy or being ill is quite difficult to define. It is affected by a number of things, including our ideas about:

- how we normally feel
- how we could feel
- what is the cause of our present condition
- how we think other people feel
- how other people respond to us
- how our friends, family and culture describe our symptoms, behaviour and feelings.

For example, if I drink too much alcohol on a Friday night then I might feel very unwell on Saturday morning, but am I ill? I know that I have brought on my own condition and that I will feel better fairly quickly. I also know that I will receive no sympathy for my condition and that I will be expected to carry out my normal tasks. In fact, I might feel much worse than when I have a heavy cold, but when I have a cold I describe myself as being ill, and I receive sympathy, Lemsip and time off from work and other responsibilities (the last point applies to males only!). So, although I feel worse with a drink-reaction than I do with a cold, I describe myself as 'ill' with the cold and not with the drink.

Another confusing example is provided by chronic disorders, for example insulin-dependent diabetes. This is a life threatening disorder, but one which can be successfully controlled so that diabetics can lead active and normal lives, with the exception that they have to take regular insulin injections. Can a diabetic be healthy? If we define good health as being the absence of any disease or physical disorder, then the answer must be 'no', but most diabetics lead very healthy lives. Clearly, defining health and illness is not going to be easy.

ARE WE GETTING HEALTHIER?

Are we getting healthier as a nation? If we take life expectancy as a measure, then the answer is yes. A child born in 1998 has a longer life expectancy (boys, 75.1 years; girls, 80.0 years) than a child born in 1984 (boys, 71.8; girls, 77.6) (DoH, 2001b). On the other hand, if we take reports of general health and longstanding sickness (NHS Executive, 1999), then the number of people in Britain who describe themselves as being in good or very good health is declining, and the number of people with at least one longstanding illness is rising (40 per cent in 1993, 44 per cent in 1999). So what does all this mean? We appear to be taking more medicines and receiving more treatment than ever, but we report more illness. One explanation for the rise in ill health is that better healthcare means that people live longer, and as people get older they have more health problems. It seems as if health workers are making work for themselves.

DEFINING 'HEALTH'

The word **health** comes from an Anglo-Saxon term meaning 'wholeness'. The same root-word gives us the words 'whole' and 'holy'. It is interesting that the religious idea of being spiritually holy has a similar origin to the medical notion of being physically healthy. Before the development of modern Western medicine the role of physical healing was often closely connected with the role of spiritual healing, and religious people were involved in the care of the sick. In many parts of the world today, spiritual health is still associated with physical health.

If we are looking for a modern definition of health, then a commonly quoted example was provided by the World Health Organisation in 1946: 'a state of complete physical, mental, and social well-being and ... not merely the absence of disease or infirmity'.

The strength of this definition is that it acknowledges that there is more to health than getting rid of spots, rashes and pains. However, when I look at that definition I am inclined to think that I have never had a day of good health in my life. It suggests that I should be in a state of 'complete' well-being, and that is rather difficult to achieve. The definition suggests that to be healthy, people must live in good social, political and economic conditions, and must be able to love, work and create. However, for many people in the world, daily life is about getting by, rather than aspiring to a state of complete well-being. Another problem with the World Health Organisation definition is that it suggests that people who are not fulfilled in life, or people who engage in dissent and live rebel lifestyles are all somehow not healthy.

THE WELLNESS CONTINUUM

It would seem that a clear definition of health and illness is not possible. There is, however, general agreement that health is not just the absence of illness. There is also general agreement that the attempt to categorise people as 'sick' or 'healthy' is not particularly helpful. Instead it is suggested that we place people somewhere on a wellness continuum (see Figure 0.1). This continuum acknowledges that nearly everyone could improve their health, and the health of every living person can also deteriorate. If we can place ourselves on the continuum then we can set about trying to improve our health and prevent illness.

Premature death / The Wellness Continuum / Optimal wellness

• **Figure 0.1:** The wellness continuum. Where would you place yourself on this continuum today?

It is not easy to define health and illness. Among other things they depend on our expectations of life, and when if these are raised, our perception of good health changes.

Models of health

When we think of healthcare, some of the first images that spring to mind are of doctors and nurses dashing around high-tech hospitals pushing trolleys loaded up with machines that go 'ping!'. Health is usually associated with doing something *physical* to the patient, such as cutting something out of the body, or administering some chemicals. This is at the heart of the **biomedical model** of health. This model has been the cornerstone of Western medicine for 300 years and it is based on the idea that illness can be explained by looking at the workings of the body, such as biochemical imbalances or abnormalities in the activity of the nervous system.

THE BIOMEDICAL MODEL

The biomedical model asks us to look at people *as if* they are biological machines. If something is going wrong then we need to fix the machine in the same way we might fix a car. We make observations and diagnose the faulty bit, then we can repair it if possible, or replace it if necessary. Sometimes we might benefit from a general overhaul and sometimes from some minor adjustments. This biomedical model has some appeal because we are clearly made up of biological bits, and also because some biomedical treatments produce dramatic improvements in health.

The biomedical model has a number of key features:

1. Reductionism
   The model tries to *reduce* explanations of illness to the simplest possible process. For example, it will look for explanations in disordered cells rather than psychological or social processes.
2. Single-factor causes
   The biomedical model looks for *the* cause of a disorder rather than looking for a range of contributory factors. For example, there are numerous attempts to explain complex disorders in terms of a simple genetic effect. Also, there is a tendency to describe smoking as the cause of coronary heart disease, yet many smokers do not develop the disease and many non-smokers do. The process would seem to have more than one cause and more than one contributory factor.

3. Mind–body distinction

    Dating back to the French philosopher Rene Descartes, Western science has made a distinction between the mind and the body. In some ways this is a religious distinction and encourages us to see people as split into two parts – a ghost and a biological machine. (This is often referred to as the 'Cartesian dualism' – Cartesian after Descartes, and dualism because it proposes a split into two). In many ways this is a comforting idea, especially when someone we love changes their personality and behaviour due to their poor health. For example, when someone develops Alzheimer's disease they become unrecognisable from the person they were throughout much of their life. It is comforting to think that the original person is still there but trapped in a decaying body.

4. Illness not health

    'If it ain't broke don't fix it' might well be the motto of the biomedical model. It deals with illness and the development of illness rather than the promotion of good health.

Theme link (**reductionism**)

Reductionism is the attempt to explain complex behaviour in terms of simple causes. There are a number of reductionist approaches in psychology including behaviourism and physiological psychology. In the case of physiological psychology, it is the attempt to explain what we do and think and feel in terms of brain structure and brain chemicals. So a person in love may poetically think 'My heart goes ping when I think of you', but according to physiological psychologists it is just their love-neurones (made-up name) firing. With this analysis, we seem to lose something of a very special human experience by reducing it to a series of chemical changes. On the other hand, however, the reductionist explanations are very plausible and this is shown by how often people are given chemicals (such as tranquillisers) to change their mood or their behaviour.

Physiological psychology gives us some suggested answers to the big question for psychologists – what is a person? The hard-line reductionist answer is that we are merely the sum of our chemicals and nerves. Any other answer begs further questions. If you argue that you have free will and can make choices about your behaviour, then where does this free will come from, and who operates it?

THE CHANGING VIEW OF HEALTH

There are three main changes that have led to dissatisfaction with the bio-medical model. First, throughout the twentieth century there was a decline in the incidence of infectious, single cause diseases. In this country at the beginning of the twentieth century, the three most common causes of death were:

1. Influenza and pneumonia
2. Tuberculosis
3. Gastro-enteritis

These are all caused by micro-organisms and respond to better living conditions and relatively simple medical interventions such as antibiotics. On the other hand, in 1999, the two illness that accounted for 64 per cent of all deaths in the UK (Office for National Statistics, 2001) were:

1. Heart disease
2. Cancer

Neither of these has a known simple cause, and the medical interventions are often drastic and costly, and have only limited success. The general picture is that large-scale infections (caused by simple micro-organisms such as bacteria) which were common in the early part of the twentieth century have been replaced by chronic diseases (such as cancer) which have multiple causes.

Secondly, there has been a dramatic increase in specialist technology and an equally dramatic increase in the cost of healthcare. The costs of treating someone who is ill are now prohibitively high so there is a major incentive to prevent people getting ill in the first place. The third change is a growing emphasis on quality of life. People are developing an expectation that they should have a healthy, enjoyable and active life. These three factors have changed the general view of health from one where we deal with illness to one where we promote good health.

It is important to add that this description of the changing priorities of health only applies to the technologically advanced countries. In other parts of the world, infectious diseases still cause many deaths despite there being relatively easy and cheap medication for them. For example, Tuberculosis (TB) was a major cause of death world wide until the development of a near perfect cure about 35 years ago. The entire course of this treatment (which is known as 'directly observed treatment short-course' or DOTS) can cost as little as £10. However, the estimated incidence of TB in the world is still 8 million cases with 3 million deaths every year, mainly in the developing world (Donaldson and Donaldson, 2000).

THE BIOPSYCHOSOCIAL MODEL

An alternative approach to the biomedical model is look at all the biological, psychological and social factors that are associated with health and illness. This is referred to as the **biopsychosocial model**. It is a real mouthful of a name, but it does have the advantage of telling you exactly what it refers to.

In contrast to the biomedical model, the biopsychosocial model is not reductionist. Instead it looks at all levels of explanation from the micro-level (for example, changes in body chemicals) to the macro-level (for example, the culture that someone lives within). The biopsychosocial model does not look for single causes but starts from the assumption that health and illness have many causes, and also produce many effects. The model does not make the distinction between mind and body but instead looks at the connections between mental events and biological changes. Finally, the biopsychosocial model is concerned as much with health as it is with illness.

The biopsychosocial model is a **systems theory**. This means that it recognises there are a number of different systems at all levels of organisation and these systems are linked. The diagram in Figure 0.2 shows some of the systems involved in human life. At one end of the scale we exist within an

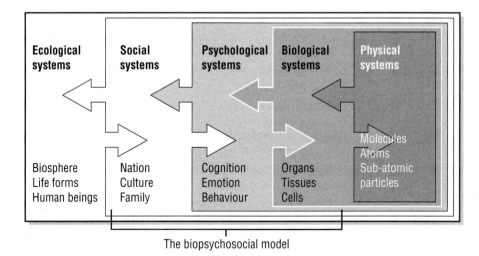

The biopsychosocial model

• **Figure 0.2:** Systems

ecological system which includes the planet we live on, the life we have developed from and the species we are part of. At the other end of the scale we are made up of the basic units of the universe – molecules, atoms and various sub-atomic particles with a range of dodgy names.

In between these two systems, the biopsychosocial model looks at three systems which are all separate from each other yet are also connected to each other – systems within systems. We live within a *social system* that includes our country our culture and our family. We also experience a *psychological system* of cognitions, emotions and behaviour and we are affected by a *biological system* of organs, tissues and cells.

One biological system that has received a lot of attention from psychologists and physicians is the **immune system** which is a collection of responses that allow the body to neutralise, eliminate or control the factors that produce disease. It seems possible that there are connections between the immune system and the experience of stress, which would fit into our psychological systems. The experience of stress is also affected by the social systems we live in, for example our family. When we look at it this way, we can see there is no *single cause* for ill health that brings out a *simple response*, but instead there are a mass of connections that create a complex series of changes within us.

The development of this biopsychosocial view of health and illness moves the emphasis away from traditional Western medicine and towards psychology. However, before we get to the psychology we will look at how changes in social policy have also brought psychology into focus.

THE NATIONAL HEALTH SERVICE

The creation of the **National Health Service** as we know it is commonly dated to the Beveridge Report of 1942. This report was carried out during the Second World War (1939–45) and formed the basis of the modern welfare state. Beveridge's proposal for a compulsory social security system was based on three assumptions:

(a) there would be a policy for keeping a high level of employment
(b) a system of children's allowances, and
(c) a comprehensive health service.

After the war, the Labour Party was swept to power with a large majority and set about creating this welfare state. Of the five key pieces of legislation, the National Health Service Act of 1946 created a comprehensive health service available to all citizens. The National Health Service came into existence on the 5th July 1948, at which time the Ministry of Health became responsible for providing this comprehensive health service.

Since its creation, the National Health Service has been through numerous reorganisations as it attempts to deal with the changing needs and aspirations of the population. It has also grown to the point where it is the largest employer in Europe with just under one million staff (782,000 whole-time equivalent) and spends around £40 billion each year (DoH, 2001b). There are a number of factors influencing change in the NHS including:

(a) advances in medical science and technology which often introduce expensive treatments and procedures
(b) demographic trends which, for example, are currently showing an change in the age profile of the population
(c) innovations in service delivery, such as NHS Direct
(d) shifts in people's expectations.

THE UNDESERVING SICK?

One of the questions for the NHS and ourselves is to decide what sort of healthcare services should be provided by the service and who should receive them. Some of the earliest attempts at **welfare** during the 17th century divided people into the deserving and undeserving poor. That is, people who were worthy of support because their condition was no fault of their own, and people who were not worthy of support because they had contributed to their current circumstances.

In the same way, the NHS has to deal with an underlying debate about the deserving and undeserving sick. For example, if someone continues to smoke cigarettes after receiving treatment for a heart condition, should the NHS fund further treatment for their condition or should it prioritise someone who is trying to take better care of their health? There is no easy answer to this, but the NHS has to deal with issues of natural justice as well as personal health. Since its creation over fifty years ago, questions have never gone away about what the NHS should be doing and how it should be doing it.

OUR HEALTHIER NATION

In 1999 the British government published a strategy for public health entitled 'Saving Lives: Our Healthier Nation' (DoH, 1999). This strategy has two main goals – to improve health, and to reduce the **health gap** (health inequalities).

The strategy builds on earlier work and widens the focus of healthcare. It recognises that although lifestyle decisions are important (for example the Banyard 'Lard & TV' Diet), there are a number of other important factors that affect health – including poverty, social exclusion, employment, housing, education and the environment. The strategy also notes that although life expectancy has gradually been increasing, the unhealthy years at the end of life have also been increasing.

The strategy emphasises disease prevention and health promotion whilst acknowledging that improvements in treatment are also important. It identifies four priorities and establishes national targets for 2010. The priorities are:

- coronary heart disease and stroke
- cancers
- mental health
- accidents.

The striking thing about this list is that the route to improvement in all the priorities is psychological. Two of the main **risk factors** with coronary heart disease and stroke are diet and smoking. These factors are also important in the development of some cancers. A further behavioural issue with cancers is encouraging people to attend for screening (see Chapter 6). One of the targets for mental health is to reduce the incidence of suicide, and this is also psychological rather than medical. The issue with accidents is to understand why some environments are more dangerous than others, and why some people are more susceptible to accidents than others (see Chapter 8). These health priorities require changes in behaviour rather than new treatments by doctors, and this leads us to look at psychology and see how it can be applied to health.

> To understand healthcare we need to consider the social, biological and psychological features that contribute to the biopsychosocial model. We also need to see the political influences on the development of healthcare in our society.
>
> **Section summary**

Psychology and health

Psychology has two special features that it brings to the study of health. The first feature is the breadth of the subject. Within the same university department you might find one psychologist strapping magnets to a pigeon's head to see if it can navigate without information about the earth's magnetic fields, and another psychologist exploring the various behaviours associated with opening and closing doors. The study of health requires us to consider a broad range of issues and consider evidence from a wide range of sources.

The second important feature of psychology is its methodology. Psychology has one hundred years of experience in trying to record and measure human behaviour and experience, and it has developed a wide range of useful methods that can be applied to health issues. In order to understand how we develop a wide range of illnesses we need to discover the following information – what do people do?, why do they do it?, how do they explain their behaviour?, and what would encourage them to change their behaviour? These are the sort of questions that psychologists have always been concerned with, so it has been a natural progression for them to become more involved in health.

The changing role of psychology in health was brought into sharper focus with the discovery of HIV/AIDS in the early 1980s. This disease poses a challenge for psychologists. Put bluntly, if you never have sex, and you never take intravenous drugs, and you never have blood transfusions, then, provided your mother was not infected when she carried you, you will not get AIDS. Solved that one then! Well, not quite, but the message is clear: you have to do something to get AIDS, and this is where psychologists come in. The disorder is transmitted behaviourally, and once you have the infection there is, as yet, no known cure. So, if we are to slow down the spread of HIV/AIDS, then we must change our behaviour and the behaviour of other people.

HEALTH PSYCHOLOGY

Health psychology has developed as an area of research within psychology. It is very different from the traditional areas, because instead of focusing on more and more detailed issues, it takes particular health problems and looks at the range of psychology that can be applied. Health psychology is defined as the:

> educational, scientific, and professional contributions of the discipline of psychology to the promotion and maintenance of health, the prevention and treatment of illness, the identification of etiology and diagnostic correlates of health, illness and related dysfunction, and the improvement of the healthcare system and health policy formation. (Matarazzo, 1982, p.4)

Health psychology provides a basis for making sense of isolated and confusing bits of data. For example, it is difficult for doctors to understand why a large proportion of patients fail to adhere to certain aspects of their treatment programmes. Models from social psychology throw some light on this and suggest ways of responding to it.

Health psychology can provide models that point to new research areas and lead to interventions that improve the practice of health behaviour or the adjustment to illness. Health psychology also takes the position that all stages of health and illness are affected by biological, psychological and social factors – the biopsychosocial model.

PSYCHOLOGY, HEALTH AND DIVERSITY

Psychology often deals with average scores rather than individual experiences. When you open a textbook it is likely to make statements about people as if we are all the same. It is important to balance this approach with evidence about the differences between individuals and the differences between groups of people. In the area of health, there are large differences in health between men and women, between different ethnic groups, and between people with different amounts of wealth.

In a society like Britain that is predominantly white but has substantial ethic minority groups, the particular health needs of these minority groups may go unnoticed by health professionals. This can have tragic consequences. Torkington (1991) describes a number of cases where people received psychiatric treatment, not because they were psychiatrically disturbed but because they were black. In one case a 51-year-old black man was rushed to hospital in Merseyside with convulsions and severe leg pains. The doctors said there was nothing wrong with him and the staff called in a psychologist. The man was put in an acute psychiatric ward where he was unattended and died one hour later of a medical complaint. The symptoms were not recognised by the health workers and the man's behaviour was not seen as a sign of physical distress but of mental disturbance. The problem is that health workers are not always familiar with the way people who are not like them behave, and are therefore likely to misinterpret that behaviour.

Theme link to Perspectives and Issues (**ethnocentrism**)

In our everyday lives we are asked to make judgements about people and events. In our judgements we are often inclined to show a little egocentrism (seeing things from our own particular viewpoint to the exclusion of others). Another bias that can be identified in our judgements is **ethnocentrism** (seeing things from the point of view of our ethnic group). This bias means that we tend to believe that the things that happen to us are the things that happen to all people, and we tend to ignore the experiences of people who are not like us.

Ethnocentrism can make us blind to the experiences of people who are not like us. Ethnocentrism also leads people to help members of their own community, and in some cases to actively disadvantage people in other communities. Racism is a feature of everyday life in Britain, and the experience of being racially abused or attacked, and the fear of these events, is a major stress factor in the lives of many people from minority cultures in this country.

THE HEALTH NEEDS OF MINORITIES

Relatively little has been written about the health needs of minority groups or their experiences in using the health service, and we have very little information about the risk factors associated with cultural difference. As a result, the health of ethnic minorities has been largely ignored or unrecognised. There are two main reasons why this state of affairs has developed in this country:

(i)   When mass immigration from the Caribbean and Asia began in this country after the Second World War (1939–1945), concerns were expressed that 'new' immigrants would bring disease into the country and create the risk of epidemics. Research, however, failed to support this and so the health service lost interest in ethnic health.

(ii)   Changing view of ethnic minorities: as the incoming ethnic groups became established in Britain, they were no longer seen as newcomers or classic immigrants. Instead they were viewed as just another part of the community without any specific needs.

What this means is that, as far as health is concerned, people from ethnic minorities are invisible. The health service has been relatively unaware of their health needs and lifestyles, and therefore unable to deal with many specific problems that they might have. McNaught (1987) argues, however, that people from ethnic minorities do have specific needs.

The health needs of minority ethnic groups in the UK were surveyed by the British government (DoH, 2001a) and some wide variations were discovered in the incidence of illness and the usage of the health service. For example, it was found that Pakistani men had an incidence of cardio-vascular disease (CVD) that was 60 per cent above the national average, while Chinese men had an incidence 35 per cent below the national average. Black Caribbean men reported much lower levels of angina but much higher levels of stroke than the national average. Among the many other findings it was discovered that diabetes was more common than the average in both males and females in the Pakistani, Bangladeshi, Indian, Chinese and black Caribbean communities.

Information on the health and illness profile of ethnic groups will allow health professionals to get a better understanding of the risk factors for various conditions, and to target treatments and health promotion programmes for different communities to achieve the appropriate changes in behaviour. The challenge for psychology is to develop explanations and interventions that include all the diverse groups of people in our society and the diverse lifestyles that people live.

End note

An evaluation of the patterns of improvements in health during the 20th century suggests that we have overestimated the effect of medicine. Diseases were in decline even before the arrival of specific medicines and we can put a lot of the improvements in health down to the general improvements in living conditions. At the start of the 21st century we can observe the effects of behaviour on health and illness, but it is important not to overestimate these effects and make claims for psychology that we can never hope to live up to.

KEY TERMS

biomedical model
biopsychosocial model
ethnocentrism
health
health gap
health psychology
immune system
National Health Service
reductionism
risk factors
systems theory
welfare
wellness continuum

EXERCISE 1

Try to identify the characteristics of health and illness as suggested in Table 0.1.

EXERCISE 2

Make a list of health conditions that you think should *not* be dealt with by the National Health Service. For example, you might think that some types of cosmetic surgery should not be available. Have a look at your list and try and work out why you included these items and not others. Alternatively you can show the list to someone else and have a heated debate.

Further reading

For more discussion of cultural issues in psychology you could look at
Moghaddam, F.M., Taylor, D.M., & Wright, S.C. (1993) *Social psychology in a cross-cultural perspective*. New York: W.H. Freeman.

For more background on health and the health services you might read
Hardey, M. (1998) *The social context of health*. Buckingham: Open University Press.

Websites

Where better to start than two general sites that have bucketloads of links and information. The World Health Organisation (WHO) and the Department of Health both provide a lot of information on the internet:
www.who.int
www.doh.gov.uk

For some academic articles you can go the British Medical Journal site at:
www.bmj.com

The patient–practitioner relationship

one

Introduction

If we want treatment we have to talk to someone about our symptoms. The interaction between us and the health worker will have an effect on the kind of treatment we receive. This chapter looks at how we interact with health workers, how they make diagnoses, and some of the factors that affect the way we use health services. These events are not as well understood as you might imagine and there are a number of questions that psychologists need to consider.

IN THIS CHAPTER WE WILL EXAMINE:

- patient and practitioner interpersonal skills
- patient and practitioner diagnosis and style
- using and misusing health services.

These questions are important in our understanding of health, and psychology has something to offer on all of them.

Patient and practitioner interpersonal skills

COMMUNICATION

Communicating is one of the basic features of being alive. We communicate all the time, often without meaning to and sometimes without knowing it. We can no more stop communicating than we can stop breathing. Even just standing still and saying nothing communicates something about our attitude and mood. If we look at the **communication** between two people then we can see three elements: the message sender, the message itself, and the message receiver (see Figure 1.1). The interesting thing for psychologists is

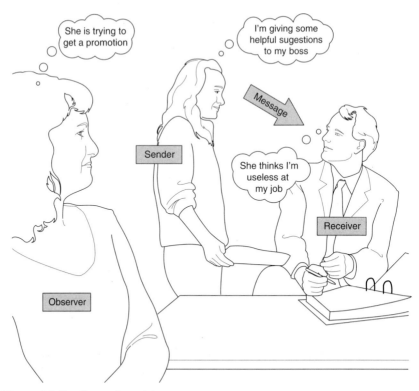

• **Figure 1.1:** Sending and receiving a message

the different understanding that the sender and the receiver may have of the same message.

NON-VERBAL COMMUNICATION

One area of communication that has attracted the attention of psychologists is **non-verbal behaviour**. This is very important in any social interaction and some psychologists (for example Argyle, 1975) suggest that it is four times as powerful and effective as verbal communication. This suggests that if we are with someone who is saying one thing, but their words do not match their facial expression or body posture, then we are more likely to believe our intuitions about their posture than we are to believe their words. For example, we might say 'Gavin told me that he likes my work, but I know he really thinks it's duff'. The power of non-verbal communication (NVC) has been recognised for years, and skilled users such as advertisers, politicians and con-artists have been able to make their words appear more convincing through their gestures and mannerisms.

Non-verbal communication is a general term used to describe communication without the use of words. Argyle (1975) suggests that non-verbal behaviours have four major uses:

1. to *assist speech* – they help to regulate conversation by showing when you want to say something, and they emphasise meaning
2. as *replacements for speech* – for example a gesture, such as a raised eyebrow, might make a verbal question unnecessary
3. to *signal attitudes* – for example we might try to look cool and unworried by taking up a relaxed standing position
4. to *signal emotional states* – we can usually tell when someone is happy, sad or tense by the way they are sitting or standing.

Non-verbal communication is an important part of the interaction between health workers and patients, but it would be untrue to suggest that we can define what all the different gestures mean. Magazine articles and books that attempt to say what gestures mean can be very misleading because there are variations in non-verbal behaviour in different cultural groups, different age groups, and between men and women.

NVC IN THE CONSULTATION

It is important in a medical consultation that there should be a good rapport between the health worker and the patient. One of the first things that we notice and make judgements about in any social situation is what people look like, so it is probably important to take account of these first impressions. McKinstry and Wang (1991) showed pictures of doctors to patients attending surgeries. The pictures were of the same male or female doctor, dressed either very formally (traditional white coat over suit or skirt), or very informally (jeans and open-necked, short-sleeved shirt, or pink trousers, jumper and gold earrings). The patients were asked to rate how happy they would be to see the doctor in each picture, and how much confidence they would have in the doctor's ability. The traditionally dressed doctors received higher preference ratings than the casually attired ones, particularly on the part of older and professional-class patients. Look at the different appearances in Figure 1.2 on p.22.

Appearance, though, isn't the only source of non-verbal communication. Argyle (1975) emphasised that all the various types of non-verbal communication interact with each other, so dress alone will not be enough to create a good communication between doctor and patient. A formally dressed doctor who avoids eye contact and doesn't use appropriate facial expressions is likely to come across as aloof or distant, and this in itself is likely to be a barrier to effective patient–doctor interaction for most people.

IMPROVING COMMUNICATION

It is possible that psychology can encourage health workers to communicate more effectively and to be attentive to the needs of their patients. Taylor (1999) suggests that this has not been dealt with in the training of doctors for three

• **Figure 1.2:** Acceptable dress for doctors: Which of these people would you accept as a doctor and which would you be cautious of?

main reasons. Firstly, there is no general agreement on what are the main features of a good consultation. The same doctor can appear remote and distant to one patient, yet another patient will describe her as 'someone I can talk to'. Secondly, there is a belief within the medical profession that good communication may make the doctor too sensitive and therefore not tough enough to deal with the difficult daily decisions of being a doctor. Thirdly, there is the argument that it is difficult enough for doctors to stay on top of all the medical information they need without complicating their lives with having to be nice to patients. However, as DiMatteo and DiNicola (1982) point out, many of the failures in medical communications stem from a lack of basic courtesy. Simple things like addressing people by their name, saying hello and goodbye and telling them where to hang their coat will only add a few moments to a consultation but will appear warm and supportive to the patient.

IMPROVING UNDERSTANDING

A major problem in the communication between patient and doctor is the different understandings and expectations they have about health and illness. In a review of this area, Ley (1989) found that a substantial proportion of patients are dissatisfied with the information they are given by health workers. In 21 surveys of hospital patients the average proportion of dissatisfied patients was 41 per cent, and for general practice patients the average proportion dissatisfied was 28 per cent. Ley attributes much of this dissatisfaction to patients not understanding or forgetting what they are told, and also to their reluctance to ask questions of health workers.

Studies on the understandings of patients often show a discrepancy between patient understandings and the current view of the medical profession. For example, people with peptic ulcers knew that acid caused ulcers, but only 10 per cent were able to correctly identify that this acid is secreted by the stomach. Also, many patients with hypertension believed, incorrectly, that they could be cured by short-term treatment (for a review see Ley, 1989). Other studies have investigated patients' knowledge about the organs of the body, and Boyle (1970) found that only 42 per cent could identify the location of the heart, 20 per cent the stomach and 49 per cent the liver. This means that over half the population are unsure where their major organs are. If people do not know where things are or what they do, it is easy to see how they can be baffled by medical explanations. (See also Chapter 2 on improving adherence rates).

not all doctors are the same

Health workers can adopt a range of styles when they interview a patient. One way of describing the differences is to characterise the style in terms of whether it is doctor-centred or patient-centred. If it is **doctor-centred** then it emphasises the imbalanced power relationship between doctor and patient, with the doctor leading the discussion by asking for medical 'facts' and giving advice. The patient on the other hand just provides the information about their complaint in response to the questions. This level of control can be seen in studies of general practice consultations where, for example, an observation of the first 90 seconds of consultations found that only 23 per cent of patients were allowed to finish their answer to the doctor's first question. In fact, the majority of these interruptions occurred in the first 15 seconds of the patient's response, and they were rarely allowed to complete their answer later on (Beckman and Frankel, 1984).

If the relationship is **patient-centred**, however, there is more emphasis placed on the patient and their unique individual needs. In this kind of discussion, the doctor tries to discover the patient's concerns and needs, and adjust their responses to match. A summary of these two styles can be found in Edlemann (2000) and is shown in Table 1.1.

• **Table 1.1:** Doctor-centred and patient-centred communication styles (adapted from Edelmann, 2000)

DOCTOR-CENTRED	PATIENT-CENTRED
Doctor's approach is based around status and control	Doctor aims to find out the patient's concerns and needs and adjust their responses to match
Doctor mainly gathers information	Doctor listens and reflects
Doctor asks: direct questions closed questions about medical 'facts'	Doctor acts by: offering observations seeking patient's ideas encouraging clarifying indicating understanding
Doctor acts by: making decisions instructing the patient	Doctor acts by: involving the patient in the decisions
Patient is expected to: be passive ask few questions not influence the consultation	Patient is expected to: be active ask questions influence the consultation

Although it might appear that all patients would prefer the patient-centred approach, this is not necessarily the case. For example, elderly patients or patients who are very sick may benefit from the confident, paternalistic approach of the doctor-centred style. Also, although patients want information about diagnosis, treatment and prognosis, they often do not want to be involved in treatment decisions (Benbassat *et al.*, 1998). This appears to be especially the case for people with life threatening disorders. Blanchard *et al.* (1988) found that although most of the cancer patients they studied wanted to receive information about their condition, only two-thirds actually wanted to participate in treatment decisions.

influences on doctor–patient discussions

So many things affect the interaction between two people that it is difficult to know where to start when we consider doctor–patient discussions. Some of the factors that have been shown to affect medical consultations include:

➤ Characteristics of the health worker: For example, gender. In a study of taped consultations with over 500 chronic disease patients and their 127 doctors (101 male, 26 female), Roter *et al.* (1991) found that female doctors talked more during the consultations than their patients. They also showed more positive talk, more partnership building, more question asking and more information giving.

➤ Characteristics of the patient: For example class, gender and age. Reviews of the various studies on this issue (for example Roter and Hall, 1992) conclude that people from the professional classes and people with more education have longer consultations and receive more information.
➤ Situational factors: For example, the number of patients on the doctor's list and the level of acquaintance between the doctor and the patient.

> **Section summary**
>
> Communication between patient and practitioner is an important aspect of healthcare. It is made difficult by many factors, including the different experiences, expectations and style of language that health workers use compared to the general public.

Patient and practitioner diagnosis and style

MAKING JUDGEMENTS AND DECISIONS

Psychologists have carried out a lot of research on the way that we make judgements and decisions. The topic is often discussed under the heading of '**human reasoning**' but this is misleading because it implies that we think in very logical ways. The reality is that there are a number of influences on the way we think and make judgements, and it is these influences and biases that are of most use in the study of health decisions.

Theme link (**cognitive psychology**)

Cognitive psychology is an approach that focuses on the way we perceive the world and process information. One aspect of this approach is to look at the ways in which we think and make decisions. This approach concentrates on the way we think rather than how we feel or behave. An example of this approach is the study of heuristics.

Every day we make judgements about probabilities. For example, we might decide not to put on a coat when we go out because we don't think it is very likely to rain. People appear to use rules for working out these probabilities and these rules are called **heuristics**. One of these rules is the **availability heuristic**, which involves judging the probability that something will happen based on the availability or prominence of the information about it. In the area of health, we tend to overestimate our chances of getting a serious disease. Serious diseases come quickly to mind because they are more frightening and also because nowadays they form a regular part of television drama. As a result of this prominence we overestimate our chances of getting these diseases. The bias that comes from the availability heuristic might affect our judgements about how risky certain behaviours are, and it might affect the diagnostic decision that health professionals make.

Another heuristic that can have an affect on health decisions is the **representative heuristic**. We make judgements about individuals and events based on what we think is typical for that group of people or that class of events. For example, if you are a smoker and you develop a medical problem, it is likely that your friends and your doctor will be inclined to attribute your medical problems to your smoking. However, even though your smoking will affect some aspects of your health, it will not be responsible for every medical condition that you develop. This is an example of how the representative heuristic can affect medical judgement.

MAKING A DIAGNOSIS

The doctor (or other health worker) has to discover what signs and symptoms the patient has, make a **diagnosis** of the problem, and then suggest the best treatment. This is not as easy as it sounds because it is not always obvious which are the important signs and symptoms, and which are the irrelevant ones. One of the problems that might affect diagnosis is the **primacy effect**. This effect is recognised in a number of areas of psychology and refers to the tendency to remember and give extra importance to the first piece of information you hear. So the first thing you tell the doctor might have a bigger effect on the diagnosis than information that comes out later in the consultation. Wallston (1978, cited in Pitts 1991a) found that doctors distorted the information that was given later in the consultation so that it fitted in with the diagnosis they made in the earlier part.

When they are examining and interviewing a patient, doctors have a limited time to obtain the information and make a diagnosis. This is made more difficult by our reluctance to tell the doctor what is really wrong with us. A study by Korsch et al. (1968) found that as many as a quarter of the mothers attending a paediatric (child) outpatient clinic failed to tell the doctor their major concern. This point is also emphasised by the effectiveness of the 'computer doctors' (see below).

The doctor must come up with a number of possible hypotheses about the condition of the patient, and, according to Weinman (1981), the choice of these hypotheses will be affected by:

1. the doctor's *approach to health* – for example, the importance they give to psychological explanations, biological explanations or social explanations of the condition

2. the *probability* of having a certain disease – this is affected by the various *heuristics* mentioned above
3. the *seriousness* of the disease and its *treatability* – for example if a disease is easily treated, and the consequences of not treating it are life-threatening, then it would be a good choice to treat it even if you are not positive about the diagnosis
4. *knowledge of the patient* – for example, their medical history and their pattern of visits to the doctor. A person who frequently consults their doctor is likely to be judged differently to someone who rarely consults.

Health workers only have a limited number of tricks (or treatments) at their disposal so they are likely to focus their consultations on symptoms that might fit these tricks. For example, a study of the consultations between cancer patients and their oncologist (cancer specialist) found that the doctor tended to take control of the discussion and tried to get the patient to talk about the 'right kind' of pain – that is, the pain that could be treated by radiotherapy, chemotherapy and surgery. Discussion of other types of pain was blocked by the doctor even though the clinic claimed to take a holistic approach to treatment (Rogers and Todd, 2000).

JUDGEMENTS OF RISK

One of the factors that will affect the final choice of treatment is the judgement of **risk** by the patient and by the doctor. This judgement can be influenced by a number of features, including how the information is presented. An example of how the presentation of the message can affect judgement was provided by Marteau (1990). In this study, a group of medical students was asked whether they would undergo, or whether they would advise patients to undergo, a number of medical procedures such as surgery for terminal liver disease, or termination of pregnancy if the unborn child would have haemophilia. When the risks of the procedures were presented to the medical students, they were framed in either a positive or negative way. For example, the researcher might describe the risk of undergoing an essential operation as being that the person had a 10 per cent chance of surviving surgery (positive frame) or a 90 per cent chance of dying (negative frame).

Marteau found that the way in which the information was presented affected the decisions which people made, even though logically, the chances were identical. If the procedure was phrased in an optimistic way, then the medical students were likely to make a more optimistic judgement. For example, they were more likely to choose an option which gave a 10 per cent chance of surviving, than one which gave a 90 per cent chance of dying, even though logically the two are identical (see Figure 1.3).

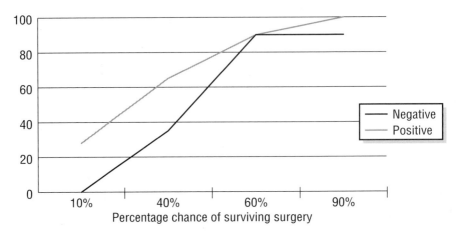

- **Figure 1.3:** Opting for medical procedures. (Source: Marteau, 1990b)

Theme link to Methodology (**self-report measures**)

A lot of our information about health comes from the **self-reports** of patients and health workers. The questions that need to be addressed are how much we can rely on this information, and what are the factors that affect the accuracy of these reports? One of these factors is the features of the person who is asking the questions. The following study shows how we give different information about our health depending on who asks us about it.

To make a diagnosis a doctor needs to know the symptoms – but do we always give the health worker a full account of our symptoms? The knowledge of the doctor and health worker can appear intimidating to the patient and make them reluctant to disclose symptoms. A study by Robinson and West (1992) illustrates this point. They were interested in the amount of self-disclosure people make when they attend a genito-urinary clinic (a clinic which specialises in venereal disease). Before they saw the doctor, patients were asked to record the intimate details of their symptoms, previous attendances and sexual behaviour on a questionnaire administered either in a written version or on a computer.

The results of the study showed that people were prepared to reveal significantly more symptoms to the computer than they would put on paper or tell the doctor (see Figure 1.4). Also, they made more disclosures about previous attendances to the computer than to the doctor. This result seems a little strange since the information you give to the doctor is personal and private, but when you are responding to a computer you have no idea how many people have access to the information. It might be that the impersonal nature of the computer allows us to come out with information of a highly personal nature. Alternatively, it might be that when we communicate with a machine we are less worried about social judgement of our sexual behaviour.

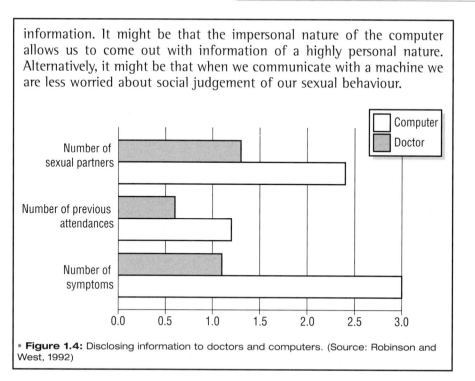

• **Figure 1.4:** Disclosing information to doctors and computers. (Source: Robinson and West, 1992)

COPING WITH A DIAGNOSIS

'Tell it to me straight, doctor, how long have I got?' is the classic line from the movies. The patient bravely asks the doctor for a direct answer, but in real life if we get a diagnosis of a chronic illness how do we respond? Shontz (1975) suggests that patients go through three stages after diagnosis: *Shock*: where the patient is stunned and bewildered and tends to act in an automated fashion while having feelings of detachment from daily life. *Encounter reaction*: where the patient has disorganised thoughts and feelings of loss, grief, helplessness and despair. *Retreat*: where the patient denies the problem and retreats into themselves.

It has to be said that these three stages are similar to the responses to **loss** described by Bowlby (for example, 1969) in attachment theory. These stages describe our immediate reaction to diagnosis, but how do we go about making sense of our illness and adjusting to it? Taylor *et al.* (1984) put forward a theory of adjustment, which was based on interviews with cardiac and cancer patients. They suggest that coping consists of three processes:

*   a search for meaning: the key questions here are 'why did it happen?' and 'what effect has it had on my life?'. Taylor *et al.* suggest that understanding the causes and implications of the illness gives it some meaning and helps the patient to cope.

- a search for mastery: the key questions are 'how can I prevent it happening again?' and 'how can I manage this?'. Answers to these questions enhance the patient's sense of control over the situation and so help the coping process.
- a process of self-enhancement: the majority of women in Taylor *et al.*'s study reported only positive changes following the diagnosis. They appeared to take the glass half full (rather than half empty) view in order to boost their self-esteem.

Section summary Diagnosis is difficult to make because of the varied ways that illnesses show up in people and the varied ways that individuals describe their symptoms. Health workers make best use of the available evidence but they may also bring their biases into the judgement process. Diagnoses are not always welcomed by the patient and there is often a long process of adjustment to the development of a chronic illness.

Using and misusing health services

USING THE HEALTH SERVICE

The most common contact between the patient and health worker is at the General Practitioner's surgery. About four-fifths of the UK population visit their GP at least once a year (86 per cent of women and 75 per cent of men), (NHS Executive, 1999), and their views of the GP's skills, attitude and ability to communicate are generally favourable. In a survey for the NHS, patients said they were generally satisfied with the length of time of their most recent **consultation**, and only 12 per cent said that the GP should have spent longer with them. Doctors tended to spend longer with older patients and therefore younger patients were more likely to be unhappy about the length of the consultation. On the down side, 15 per cent of patients said they had been put off seeking help at least once in the previous 12 months because of the inconvenience of surgery hours, and 19 per cent of patients said the receptionist had made it difficult to talk to their GP. Dissatisfaction is also shown by the finding that 11 per cent of patients said they had felt like making a complaint about someone at the surgery at least once in the previous 12 months, though only 1 per cent of cases actually led to a formal complaint.

GOING TO THE DOCTOR

We do not go to the doctor every time we feel ill. Research suggests that on the vast majority of occasions that we experience a symptom of illness, we do not report it to a health worker. We usually ask other people, most likely our family and friends, for advice before we decide to go to the doctor. These '**lay consultations**' are very common and Scambler and Scambler (1984) estimate that we make eleven lay consultations for every medical consultation. We receive advice such as: 'I went to the doctor with that and she just told me to rest', or more worryingly, 'Our Gladys had symptoms like that just before she died.' So what are the factors that encourage us to go beyond the lay consultations and visit the doctor? Pitts (1991a) suggests the following:

- *persistence of symptoms;* we are likely to take a 'wait and see' approach if we get ill and only seek medical advice if the symptoms last longer than we expect
- *critical incident;* a sudden change in the symptom or the amount of pain can encourage us to seek medical advice
- *expectation of treatment;* we are only likely to seek medical advice if we think it will do some good. If we have had the same symptoms before and not received any useful treatment then we are unlikely to bother making an appointment.

On the whole we do not go to the doctor unless we feel it is important because we think we 'should not waste their valuable time'. This perception means that many people do not seek advice even when they have developed serious symptoms. Therefore if the lay consultations do not encourage them to seek medical advice, their reluctance to go to the doctor can have serious consequences.

the mcdoctors

Our relationship with health workers is affected by the general changes within our society. Ritzer (1993) suggests that all parts of society, even the health services, are affected by the McDonalds culture. Medicine is becoming an assembly-line process, and patients are now called 'customers' or 'consumers'. We don't *receive treatment* any more, we *consume* the services of health workers. The management of the health service is concerned with efficiency, numbers of units, and through-put. They are starting to develop 'walk-in-doctors', where the patient will go to an emergency room and receive fairly speedy treatment. The emergency room deals with a limited range of disorders, but is able to deal with a lot of them and very quickly. This is like a fast-food restaurant, such as McDonalds, where the diners have a limited menu choice but know exactly what they will be getting, and know they will get it quickly.

If you walk into a modern British hospital you can see this changing style of health. The Queens Medical Centre in Nottingham, for example, has an international reputation and contains a number of high-profile specialist services, as well as medical and nursing schools. As you walk through the front door, the impression is of a shopping mall, with small shops where you can buy anything from fast-food to books. There is even a travel agent ('Only got one month to live madam? I've got a late availability bargain break just for you!'). Health is becoming just another part of our consumer behaviour, and in the process some feel it is becoming de-humanised. This will inevitably change our relationship with health workers, or to use Ritzer's term, our relationship with the McDoctors. *Have a nice day!*

delay in seeking help

We are sometimes quite reluctant to seek medical advice even when we have serious symptoms. For example, a study of 800 elderly patients with newly diagnosed cancer found that 48 per cent had sought help within two months of noticing the symptoms, 19 per cent had delayed for over three months, and 7 per cent had delayed for a year (Samet *et al.* 1988). People who experience the symptoms of heart attack commonly delay before seeking help. A study of heart attack survivors in Glasgow found that only 25 per cent had called for help when the symptoms started, and 60 per cent waited four hours before calling (MacReady, 2000). In fact, 12 per cent of the patients waited a full day before seeking help. Numerous other studies find similar results for a range of conditions, many of them life-threatening. It has to be said that delay is often an appropriate option since many symptoms disappear quite quickly, so it is difficult to know when to seek medical advice.

Delay can occur at a number of decision points en route to the surgery. Some psychologists suggest that **delay** occurs in a three-stage process (Safer *et al.* 1979):

1. appraisal delay – the time it takes for a person to interpret their symptoms as a sign of illness
2. illness delay – the time it takes between realising that you are ill and deciding to seek medical advice
3. utilisation delay – the time it takes between deciding to go, and turning up at the surgery. Different people will delay at different points in this process, and different symptoms and conditions will also bring about different patterns of response.

There are number of other factors that have been found to affect delay in seeking help, including;

- *Characteristics of the patient*
  For example, age, gender and culture. Age can have an effect because elderly people may interpret their symptoms as being part of the ageing process. When people attribute their symptoms to ageing they are more likely to delay in seeking treatment (Prohaska *et al.* 1987). Some symptoms may also be less obvious in older people. For example, they report less pain than younger people with angina, and as a result might

not seek help for an underlying heart condition (Day et al., 1987).

- *Illness-related factors*
  For example, the site of the symptoms, the type of symptoms, and the speed of development of the symptoms. Some conditions, such as sexually transmitted disease or incontinence, can create a lot of embarrassment and this may lead to delay (Leenaars et al., 1993). Also, symptoms that develop slowly or are not too severe will also lead to delay in reporting (Prohaska et al., 1987).
- *Health beliefs*
  For example, the frequency with which women examine their breasts for possible cancer is affected by their beliefs about the seriousness of the disease and their personal susceptibility to it (Ashton et al., 2001). A similar result was found for people with breathing difficulties (Abraham et al., 1999), suggesting that a sizeable number of people with this condition in the UK are not seeking help, and one of the key factors is their belief about the illness.

overuse of health services

All health services have their limits. We can't see a health worker for every ache and pain, bruise and scratch. But when should we seek help? The flip-side of delay is to go to the surgery too often or too soon. Some conditions, for example meningitis, require speedy diagnosis and prompt treatment. Delay can be fatal. Influenza, on the other hand, has to run its course for most people – there is very little that a doctor can do for an adult who normally enjoys good health other than to say 'Have a nice day!' or 'Get well soon!'

Some people worry a lot about their health and it is estimated that worried people, some who are well and some who are ill, place high demands on the health services (Wolinsky and Johnson, 1991). At the extreme end of the scale there are a few people who continue to visit their doctors even though there are no obvious signs of illness, and even when the doctor has taken all reasonable steps to reassure the patient. These patterns of abnormal illness behaviour are commonly given 'disease' labels such as **hypochondriasis**. This label, however, is commonly used in an informal way and not based on recognised tests and procedures. It is based on the health worker's belief that the patient's complaints are exaggerated or unfounded. Sadly, on some occasions, the label is made incorrectly when the health worker cannot find any explanation for the illness behaviour and comes to the conclusion that it is 'all in the patient's head'.

munchausen syndrome

A small number of people seek out excessive medical attention, often going from city to city to get new diagnoses and new surgical interventions. This is sometimes diagnosed as an illness itself – **Munchausen Syndrome**. In very exceptional circumstances, individuals seek excessive and inappropriate medical contact through the 'illness' of a relative such as a child. This can be seen as a form of child abuse, where the parent (usually a mother) exaggerates, fabricates or induces illness in their child. The main motivation is believed to be that the parent wants to show herself to be an exceptional mother. This condition is referred to as 'Munchausen by proxy'.

The most famous case of this in the UK was the nurse Beverley Allitt. Between February and April of 1991 there were 26 unforeseen failures of medical treatment and unaccountable injuries on Ward 4 of Grantham and Kesteven General Hospital. In total four children died and nine were injured. Investigations found that nurse Beverley Allitt had altered critical settings on life support equipment and administered lethal doses of potassium and insulin to children in her care (The Allitt Inquiry, 1991). She was diagnosed as suffering from Munchausen syndrome by proxy and was sentenced to thirteen concurrent life sentences.

abuses by the health services

It is worth pointing out that the misuse of health services is not all one-way. There is an argument to be made that medical services are bad for your health. In its extreme form this argument suggests that the major advances in life expectancy and good health are much more to do with the rise in living standards and public sanitation than to do with medics. Illich, in his book *Medical Nemesis* (1975), suggests that 'the medical establishment has become a major threat to health' (p.11). In fact, it is recognised that one of the most likely places to catch a new illness in the UK is in hospital (Plowman *et al.,* 2000) and **iatrogenic** (doctor-made) illness is a major cost to the health service. It is clearly not the aim of hospitals to make people ill, but Illich's argument is that the power of the medical profession makes us helpless about our own health, and gullible to intrusive treatments that have only marginal benefits or no benefits at all.

On a less philosophical but more chilling note, the power of doctors can also be abused. Most famously there is the example of Harold Shipman, the Yorkshire GP who murdered an unknown number of his elderly female patients before being convicted in January 2000. He was able to operate unchallenged for many years despite there being evidence of anomalies in his death rates, a personal history of drug abuse, and a series of complaints made against him (Ramsey, 2001). The question that arises is 'how could this happen?'. Although there are no easy answers, two of the contributing factors might be the trust invested in doctors by their patients, and the lack of monitoring within the health service and its professional associations.

Our general experience of health workers is good, but it is also fair to say that a significant number of patients have poor experiences for a variety of reasons. It is true that hospitals can make us sick, and doctors can make the wrong diagnosis, but the cost–benefit analysis suggests that healthcare in the UK contributes massively to increasing the length and enhancing the quality of life.

Section summary

KEY TERMS

availability heuristic
cognitive psychology
communication
consultation
delay
diagnosis
doctor-centred
heuristics
human reasoning
hypochondriasis
iatrogenic
lay consultation
loss
Munchausen Syndrome
non-verbal behaviour
non-verbal communication
patient-centred
primacy effect
representative heuristic
risk
self-reports

EXERCISE 1

Carry out a small-scale survey (ask your family and friends) about whether they are satisfied with the treatment they receive from their GP surgery. You might go further and ask what are the bits they like and bits they don't like about going to the surgery. You could then take the results to your doctor and watch while they strike you off their list!

EXERCISE **2**

Carry out a small study on judgement of risk. You could use a similar design to Marteau (1990) and ask whether a person should undergo an operation if they had an xx per cent chance of survival or an xx per cent chance of dying.

ESSAY QUESTION

(a) Describe what psychologists have found out about the relationship between patients and health workers.

(b) Discuss the psychological evidence on the relationship between patients and health workers.

(c) Suggest one intervention that will encourage people not to delay seeking help when they have serious symptoms. Give reasons for your suggestion.

Further reading

To find out more about doctor–patient communication you could do no better than read: Ley, P. (1988) *Communicating with patients*. London: Croom-Helm.

To look at the general psychology of making judgements then you could read: Plous, S. (1993) *The psychology of judgement and decision making*. New York: McGraw Hill.

Websites

When you are looking for health information it is important to use the web with caution. Anyone can publish information and even though it may be well presented it does not mean that it is scientifically accurate. It is always better to use sources that have been checked out by qualified doctors to ensure their accuracy. Even then, this does not mean that the information can be trusted. Some information is given out by groups or individual who may be biased as they stand to gain financially from people using the treatments or services they are promoting.

Look out for the logos of Health on the Net and OMNI which are quality
stamps to show the site meets certain standards. As well as providing
kitemarks these sites both offer a lot of information, as does NHS Direct:
www.hon.ch
www.omni.ac.uk/
www.nhsdirect.nhs.uk/

Adherence to medical advice

two

Introduction

Adherence to health requests means doing as we are told and being sensible about our health. It means taking our medicine, eating the right foods, and putting on a warm vest when we go out in winter. This all seems straightforward enough, but it appears that people don't always follow this advice.

THIS CHAPTER EXAMINES THE FOLLOWING ISSUES:

- why people don't adhere to medical advice
- measuring adherence
- improving adherence.

Why people don't adhere to medical advice

TRADITIONAL APPROACHES IN SOCIAL PSYCHOLOGY

The research on compliance that is popularly quoted in introductory psychology texts was carried out in the 1950s and 1960s with the aim of explaining why seemingly ordinary people carried out hideous acts against fellow human beings during the Second World War (1939–45). This research gives a picture of people as compliant automatons who readily conform to most social pressures and obey authority without much hesitation (see for example the work of Asch, 1955 and Milgram, 1963). In the world of health, however, the problem is very different. People do not always comply with requests from authority figures, far from it. In fact we are more likely to ignore health requests than we are to follow them.

HOW MUCH DO PEOPLE ADHERE TO HEALTH REQUESTS?

Developing an accurate picture of treatment **adherence** can be tricky, and the estimates of patient compliance vary widely from one study to another. This is partly a matter of definition. Taylor (1990), for example, suggested that 93 per cent of patients fail to adhere to some aspect of their treatment regimes, whereas Sarafino (1994) argued that people adhere 'reasonably closely' to their treatment regimes about 78 per cent of the time for short-term treatments, and about 54 per cent of the time for chronic conditions. In other words, the two researchers were using different definitions. Taylor was talking about precise adherence to every detail of the recommended treatment. Sarafino, on the other hand, was allowing for the way that most people 'customise' their treatments to fit in with their own lifestyles, but also recognising that they could still be complying with the general features of the treatment.

Sarafino also found that the average adherence rates for taking medicine to prevent illness was roughly 60 per cent for both long-term and short-term regimes, but compliance with a requirement to change one's lifestyle, such as stopping smoking or altering one's diet, was generally quite variable and often very low. There are limits, it seems, as to how far people will adhere to medical demands if they seem to involve too great a change.

A study of 350 seventy-year-olds in Denmark (Barat *et al.*, 2001) measured adherence by getting information from the individual's GP and by visiting their home, asking them some questions, and checking their medicine cupboard. They compared the information from the GP and the information from the patient and found disagreement over the medicine in 22 per cent of cases, the doses in 71 per cent of cases, and the treatment programmes in 69 per cent of cases. During questioning, 24 per cent of the elderly patients said they did not always follow the prescription, though this was commonly with low dose and less frequent use drugs. Only 60 per cent said they knew the purpose of the drugs, only 21 per cent knew the problems that would arise if they stopped taking them, and only 6 per cent knew the possible side-effects of the drugs. Patients were more likely to adhere to the treatment programme if they knew more about the drugs, and less likely to adhere if they were taking three or more prescribed drugs. This study highlights some of the many factors that affect adherence to health requests.

CUSTOMISING TREATMENT

Individuals have their own way of doing many everyday tasks. They may like to eat their food in a particular way, keep certain photos with them all the time, or organise their living room just as they want it. They are not fussy, they are just customising their lives. In a similar way, people also seem to **customise** their treatment programmes. They might consult their GP but they probably also take advice from family and friends. They might pick up health tips from magazines and television and may well choose to buy some over the counter medicines (which are not under the control of the doctor) to add to their customised healthcare programme. Older people tend to be more proactive in their healthcare and make a lot of use of over the counter medicines. A study of elderly patients in Britain suggested that their purchase of these medicines fell into four categories (Johnson and Bytheway, 2000):

- prevention and maintenance, which are mainly nutrition supplements like vitamins or products that are 'good for the blood'
- alternatives to going to the doctor, for conditions such as indigestion, skin irritations, or headaches
- supplements or replacements for prescription medicines, such as painkillers or other medicines recommended by the doctor
- items to counteract the side-effects of prescription medicines, for example laxatives to counteract the constipation caused by many painkillers.

So if we take this customising of treatment into account, are these people adhering to the health requests or not? In the strictest sense they are not, but they may well be following a programme that is right for them and makes best use of the available information.

RATIONAL NON-ADHERENCE

One of the most obvious reasons why patients do not comply with health requests is that they do not believe it is in their best interests to do so – the patient is making a rational decision not to comply. This behaviour is known as **rational non-adherence**. The patient might not believe that the treatment will help them get better, or they might believe that the treatment will cause more problems than it solves. For example, a study by Bulpitt (1988, cited in Kaplan *et al.,* 1993) on the use of treatments for hypertension found that the medication improved the condition by reducing the symptoms of depression and headache, but it also had the side-effects of increased sexual problems such as difficulty with ejaculation and impotence. For some men this would not be a price worth paying. It would therefore be a rational decision to decline to take the medication (see Figure 2.1 on p.42).

Studies on adherence rarely consider the negative outcomes of the treatment that the patient is being asked to follow, and the costs of adherence are rarely calculated. Various studies, however, have found that treatment programmes often have serious side-effects. For example, Williamson and Chapin (1980) suggest that 10 per cent of admissions to a geriatric unit were the result of undesirable drug side-effects. So if we are looking at adherence we should also consider the negative effects of the treatment and the preferences of the patient.

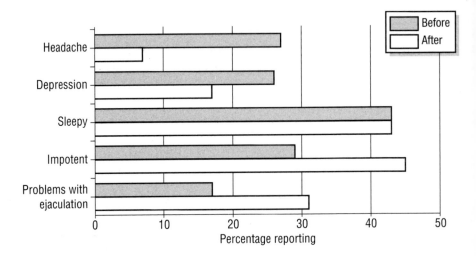

• **Figure 2.1:** Symptoms of patients with hypertension before and after treatment. Patients are only likely to adhere to the treatment if they judge that the changes have an overall benefit.

Sarafino (1994) summarises the reasons why a rational patient might not adhere to the recommended treatment:

- they have reason to believe that the treatment is not helping
- the side-effects are unpleasant, worrying or reduce their quality of life
- they are confused about when to take the treatment and how much is required
- there are practical barriers to the treatment, such as the cost of medication
- they may want to check that the illness is still there when the treatment is discontinued.

Therefore, far from being awkward or ignorant, the non-adhering patient is often making the best sense they can of their own health problem.

OTHER USEFUL CONCEPTS

There are a number of other concepts in psychology that can be used to help explain the adherence or non-adherence of patients. These include:

behavioural explanations

Learning theories offer a number of possible explanations for non-adherence. These include the role of habits, the power of imitation and the effects of reinforcement.

defence mechanisms

The psychoanalytic approach suggests that we protect our ego by a variety of means, for example, **avoidance** (smokers are known to avoid information about the harmful effects of smoking), and **denial** (this isn't really happening).

cognitive explanations

Other useful concepts include self-efficacy and locus of control. Both these concepts are discussed in Chapter 7. **Locus of control** refers to the sense of control a person feels over their situation; whether they have personal choice or whether they have little influence on what is happening. The more a person feels in control of their health and their treatment, the more likely they are to comply with the treatment programme. The concept of **self-efficacy** refers to the belief that a person will be successful in what they are trying to do. People are unlikely to follow a treatment programme if they doubt their ability to carry it out. For example, most smokers know that smoking is harmful and that quitting will improve their health. However, many smokers believe that they are not able to give up, and so do not try. If we want a patient to follow a treatment programme then we need to ensure that they believe that they are capable of carrying it out.

doctors as patients

Health workers might well raise their eyebrows at the thought of patients not following medical advice, but do the health workers follow their own advice? A survey of over a thousand British GPs and consultants (Forsythe et al., 1999) found that on the whole they did not follow the British Medical Association guidelines on the **ethical responsibilities** towards themselves and their families. For example, it is recommended that doctors do not prescribe medicines for themselves, but over 70 per cent reported that they usually or sometimes self-prescribed. Also, the BMA guidelines suggest that doctors should not treat or prescribe for the close family, yet over 80 per cent did just that. Perhaps this just confirms an old myth that doctors make the worst patients.

Section summary

We don't always do as we are told by health workers (or our mothers). At first glance this appears to be lazy or even reckless, but a closer consideration shows that many of the health choices we make are a common-sense way of dealing with the many influences on us.

Measuring adherence

TYPES OF REQUEST

One of the issues to consider with adherence is the type of behaviour we are asking someone to follow. In the social psychology studies mentioned above, the person under investigation was usually isolated from their friends and, in the Asch studies, asked to carry out simple and transparently pointless tasks. In the Milgram study they were asked to carry out something very unusual in a very unusual situation. Requests for health adherence, on the other hand, are usually made in familiar situations and the behaviour can be discussed with friends and family.

The types of health request fall into a number of categories:

1. requests for short-term adherence with simple treatments, for example 'take these tablets twice a day for three weeks'
2. requests for positive additions to lifestyle, for example 'eat more vegetables and take more exercise'
3. requests to stop certain behaviours, for example 'stop smoking'
4. requests for long-term treatment regimes, for example sticking to a diabetic diet, or the diet prescribed for people undergoing renal dialysis.

A cursory look at these types of request reveals some striking differences, and suggests that the problems of adherence might be different for the different types of medical request. For example, with the short-term request to take my tablets three times a day, I have to make an effort for a short time and even then it is unlikely to impose any strain on the way I conduct my life. On the other hand, the dietary requirements for patients undergoing renal dialysis are very severe, difficult to follow, and will continue for as long as the patient has dialysis. The diet requires the patient to severely restrict their fluid intake, which not only cuts out a Friday night down the Dog and Partridge, but also leaves them feeling thirsty and uncomfortable for much of the time.

When we talk about adherence to health requests, we need to consider what we are asking people to adhere to. It is too much of a simplification to regard all health requests as being the same. The reasons why we do not adhere to one type of request might be very different to reasons why we do not adhere to another.

Theme link to Methodology (**self-report measures/ overestimating adherence**)

When we look at the studies on adherence there are two reasons for thinking that the estimates of adherence might be a bit optimistic. The first problem is the selection of people to take part in studies. For example, a study by Riekert and Drotar (1999) compared people who participated in a study on adherence to diabetes treatment (participants) with people who failed to return the study **questionnaire** (non-returners). They found that the two groups were similar in most personal characteristics such as age and economic status, but the non-returners had lower treatment adherence scores and tested their blood sugar less frequently than the participants. This data is available because of the regular contact many diabetics have with clinics. The obvious problem for research is that we can only estimate an individual's adherence if they make themselves available for research – even if that just means answering a questionnaire.

The other problem with adherence research is that people will not always tell the truth. One of the reasons for this is to present a good impression to the health workers. This can be very important, since the patient might well believe that they will only receive the best treatment if the health staff believe that they are carrying out their instructions. An extreme example is of smokers who have been refused treatment if they admitted that they were still smoking.

MEASUREMENT TECHNIQUES

It is important to develop reliable ways of measuring adherence, and Cluss and Epstein (1985) suggest that the following methods can be used:

1. *Self-report:* Ask the patient and they may tell you how adherent they have been. Unfortunately it is a consistent research finding that patients overestimate their adherence to the treatment programme. Some studies have been able to compare a patient's report of their adherence of taking medication with blood or urine samples that record the level of medication in the body. These studies show that patients seriously overestimate their adherence.
2. *Therapeutic outcome:* Is the patient getting better? If, for example, a patient is taking medication for hypertension then we would expect their blood pressure to decrease. However, there are a range of other factors that also affect blood pressure including changes in the environment and the patient's level of stress.
3. *Health worker estimates:* Ask the doctor and they should be able to estimate how adherent a patient is being. Once again, this method has been found to be very unreliable.
4. *Pill and bottle counts:* If we count the number of pills left in the bottle and compare it with the number that ought to be there then we should get a measure of adherence. The drawback to this method is that

patients can throw the pills away, and unless we have random, unexpected raids on bathroom cabinets by crack teams of experimental psychologists, we are not much further forward than the method of self-report.

5. *Mechanical methods:* A number of devices have been developed to measure how much medicine is dispensed from a bottle. These devices are expensive and they only measure how much medicine goes out of the bottle, not how much goes into the person.

6. *Biochemical tests:* It is possible to use blood tests or urine tests to estimate how adherent a patient has been with their medication. For example, it is possible to estimate adherence with diet in renal patients by measuring the levels of potassium and urea in their blood when they report for their next session of dialysis.

Overall, we can use a wide variety of methods to investigate patient adherence, but like all methods in psychology, they only produce estimates of behaviour, and they all contain some degree of error.

A treatment that is growing in the UK is oral asthma medication, and measuring adherence rates will help us to measure the effectiveness of the medicines. If people follow the prescribed treatment programme they should reduce the attacks of breathlessness, but many people forget or decline to take the medicine regularly. A study in London used an electronic device (TrackCap) on the medicine bottle which recorded the date and time of each use of the bottle (Chung and Naya, 2000). The patients were told that adherence rates were being measured, but were not told about the details of the TrackCap. The medicine was supposed to be taken twice a day, so a person was seen as adhering to the treatment if the TrackCap was used twice in a day, 8 hours apart. Over a twelve-week period, compliance was relatively high (median 71 per cent), and if the measure was a comparison of TrackCap usages with the number of tablets then adherence was even higher (median 89 per cent).

Another study on asthma medicines, this time inhalers, checked for adherence by telephoning the patient's pharmacy to assess the refill rate (Sherman *et al.,* 2000). They calculated adherence as a percentage of the number of doses refilled divided by the number of doses prescribed. This study of over 100 asthmatic children in the USA was able to compare pharmacy records with doctor's records and with the records of the medical insurance claims for treatment. They concluded that the pharmacy information was over 90 per cent accurate and could therefore be used as basis for estimating medicine use. They also found that adherence rates were generally quite low (for example 61 per cent for inhaled corticosteroids), and that doctors were not able to identify the patients who had poor adherence.

Measuring behaviour is difficult at the best of times. Measuring behaviour such as treatment adherence, which is often done in private, is even more difficult. The various methods used, however, probably give us a fair idea of how much people follow medical advice.

Improving adherence

Psychology can help us understand why people do not adhere, or find adherence difficult, and it can help us improve adherence with treatment programmes.

One factor that might improve adherence is designing information sheets and treatment programmes that are easy to understand and carry out. An important aspect of this is to consider the special needs of different client groups. Old people, for example, often have different understandings and health beliefs to young people. Kaplan *et al.* (1993) identifies three problems for old people in following treatment programmes:

i)   Some old people have difficulty understanding and following complex instructions. Although ageing is not necessarily related to mental decline, some old people develop cognitive problems, such as memory loss, which make it more difficult to follow treatment programmes.

ii) Older people sometimes have difficulty with medicine containers because they lack the manual dexterity to deal with childproof caps. It has been noted that older people sometimes get over this problem by transferring the tablets to other containers, and this can lead to confusion about which tablet is which.

iii) Older people are sometimes on a range of medications for different conditions and these might be prescribed by different doctors. This increases the risks of unpleasant side-effects, and so increases the chance that the patient will decide to discontinue the treatment.

Looking at the above, it would appear that treatment programmes for the older patient need to take special consideration of this client group in order to improve adherence.

Theme link to Behaviourism

Behaviourism is one of the main approaches in the history of psychology. It developed from the writings of John Watson (1913) and incorporated the early work of Skinner, Pavlov and Thorndike. It focuses on what people do and looks to explain it terms of the stimuli that precede the behaviour and the rewards that follow it. The theory has developed over the last 100 years and there are many behavioural interventions that are still used. There are a number of effective behavioural approaches to adherence including:

Feedback: where the patient gets regular reports on the state of their health, and so is reinforced for their adherence behaviour.

Self-monitoring: where the patient is encouraged to keep a written record of their treatment, such as their diet or their blood–glucose levels (diabetics).

Tailoring the regime: where the treatment is customised to fit in with the habits and lifestyle of the patient.

Prompts and reminders: something that helps the patient to remember the treatment at the appropriate time, for example setting an alarm timer or receiving a reminder phone call.

Contingency contract: where the patient negotiates a contract with the health worker concerning their treatment goals and the rewards they should receive for achieving those goals.

Modelling: where the patient sees someone else successfully following the treatment programme and imitates that behaviour.

PRESENTATION OF THE INFORMATION

People will be more likely to follow the instructions for their treatment if they understand what they have to do and why they have to do it. One of the important factors here is the quality of the communication between health worker and patient (see Chapter 1 for further discussion of this). A range of training programmes for health workers has been used to improve this communication and Sarafino (1994) summarises the general findings from these studies:

- verbal instructions should be as simple as possible and should use straightforward language:
- instructions should be specific rather than general
- break complicated treatment programmes down into a series of smaller ones
- key information should be emphasised
- use simple written instructions
- get the patient to repeat the instructions in their own words.

Taylor (1986) suggests that the health worker is a very credible source who can tailor the health message to the individual needs of the patient and thus encourage adherence. The face to face nature of the interaction between patient and health worker tends to hold the attention of the patient and allows the health worker to check that the patient understands what they need to do. The health worker can also enlist the support of other family members and increase the level of social support available to the patient. Finally, the health worker has the patient under partial supervision and so they can monitor their progress and encourage them to continue with the treatment.

MEMORY

One of the problems for patients in a medical consultation is **remembering** what they have been told by the health worker. We are not very good at remembering detail at the best of times, and it is even harder to remember material that we do not understand or material that is new to us. Ley *et al.* (1973) investigated how accurately people remember medical statements. Patients attending a general practice surgery were given a list of medical statements and were then asked to recall them. The same list was also given to a group of students. The statements were either given in an unstructured way, or were preceded by information about how they would be organised. For example, a structured presentation might involve the researcher saying something like, 'I'm going to tell you three things: firstly, what is wrong with you; secondly, what tests we will be doing, and thirdly, what is likely to happen to you'.

When they were tested to see how much they remembered, Ley *et al.* found that structuring the information had made a very clear difference. The patients who had received the information in a clearly **categorised** form remembered about 25 per cent more than those who had received the same information in an unstructured way. A similar study on students, who are more used to learning information, found they remembered 50 per cent more if they received categorised information than if it were unstructured. There is clear message in these results for how information should be given to patients so that they will remember it, and this is important because if you cannot remember the instructions then you cannot adhere to them.

The study above is about list learning, but what do people remember of real consultations? Ley (1988) investigated this by speaking to people after they had visited the doctor. They were asked to say what the doctor had told them to do and this was compared with a record of what had actually been said to them. Ley found that people were quite poor at remembering medical information. In general, patients remembered about 55 per cent of what their doctor had said to them, but the inaccuracies were not random ones. Ley found the following patterns in the errors made by the patients:

- they had good recall of the first thing they were told (the **primacy effect**)
- they did not improve their recall as a result of repetition – it did not matter how often the doctor repeated the information
- they remembered information which had been categorised (e.g. which tablets they should be taking) better than information which was more general

- they remembered more than other patients if they already had some medical knowledge.

In a follow-up to the study, Ley prepared a small booklet giving advice to doctors on how to communicate more clearly with their patients. Patients whose doctors had read the booklet recalled on average 70 per cent of what they had been told, which was a significant increase on the previous figure.

TECHNICAL TERMS

People are easily baffled and intimidated by technical terms. This is particularly true in the area of health where are there numerous big words for relatively simple procedures. If you look at the following commonly used medical terms, are you confident you know what they refer to?

protein
haemorrhoid
antibiotic
virus
anti-emetic
insulin
enema

If you take the term 'virus' then this is something we might refer to in everyday conversation. 'I'm not going to work today, I've got a bit of a virus.' What does it mean to 'have a virus', and do we know what a virus is and how we should treat it?

McKinlay (1975) carried out an investigation into the understanding that women had of the information given to them by health workers in a maternity ward. The researchers recorded the terms that were used in conversations with the women and then asked them what they understood by 13 of these terms including: *breech*, *purgative*, *mucus*, *glucose* and *antibiotic*. On average, each of the terms was understood by less than 40 per cent of the women. Even more remarkable were the expectations of the health workers who used the terms. When they were asked whether they expected their patients to understand these terms their estimates were even lower than 40 per cent.

It seems that the health workers did not expect their patients to understand what they were being told, so why did they use the difficult terms? The likely answer is that medical language probably makes the health worker appear more knowledgeable and more important, and it might also make the conversation brief because the patient will not be able to ask any questions without the fear of appearing stupid. The problem is that if patients do not understand the information, or are unable to remember it, then they have little chance of adhering to the treatment programme.

It is interesting to note that the psychologist William James first wrote over 100 years ago about the unhelpful way that doctors use medical terms, referring to it as 'simple minded' and 'superficial medical talk' (Rubin, 2000). Even the most recent studies (for example, Howlett, 2000) continue to highlight the problems in finding the right words to explain medical conditions to the general public.

Our concerns about adherence are usually directed at the patient. Researchers look for reasons why the patient does not follow the treatment programme and suggest what might be done about it. The above summaries, however, suggest that one of the best ways to improve compliance is to change the behaviour of the health worker who gives the treatment instructions. If the interaction between the patient and the health worker is improved then we might see dramatic improvements in adherence rates.

DIRECTLY OBSERVED THERAPY (DOT)

The direct observation of patients taking their medicine is a strategy used to improve completion rates of tuberculosis treatment. It was first introduced over 40 years ago, and is still extensively used around the world in various formats. Adherence to the treatment programme is especially important in tuberculosis because of the seriousness of the disease, the ease with which it spreads, and the danger of the medicines becoming ineffective through resistance. A review of 32 studies of DOT programmes since 1996 found that most reported improved adherence rates – though the many extra features of the studies might well have contributed to these results (Volmink *et al.,* 2000). The extra features of the programmes included reminder letters to clinics and financial incentives. In one programme in the USA, patients received the equivalent of $100 a month to continue with the programme. This might appear generous but it should also be noted that in New York the law was changed so that people could be required to take the treatment or face compulsory admission to hospital or imprisonment. This seems to be an effective, if brutal, way of encouraging adherence. In some studies, the important factors were social variables such as friendly relationships between staff and patients. The review concludes by suggesting that many studies concentrate on DOT as the active ingredient of the adherence programme, but that it might well be that the other factors (such as incentives) have a greater effect.

Section summary   People can encouraged to be more adherent through a variety of methods. The more successful ones include improving the available information, watching people take the medicine, and threatening them with prison.

KEY TERMS

adherence
avoidance
behaviourism
categorised information
customise
denial
ethical responsibilities
locus of control
primacy effect
questionnaire
rational non-adherence
remembering
self-efficacy

EXERCISE 1

Have a look in your bathroom cabinet and read the instructions of the medicines that you find. How many have you or your housemates/family been using incorrectly? How many are out of date? Why have you been using them without reading the instructions fully?

EXERCISE 2

Use the list of technical terms on p.50 and ask people if they know what they mean.

ESSAY QUESTION

(a) Describe what psychologists have found out about why people do not follow medical advice.

(b) Discuss the psychological evidence on the reasons why people do not follow medical advice.

(c) Suggest one technique that could be used to encourage children to use their asthma inhalers more regularly. Give reasons for your answer.

Further reading

If you are interested in the problems of measuring things in health psychology then you should pick up: Karoly, P. (Ed) (1985) *Measurement strategies in health psychology*. New York: Wiley.

On the other hand, if you want to read about the social psychology of social compliance then you could try: Milgram, S. (1977) *The individual in the social world*. New York: Addison Wesley.

Websites

The Wired for Health project is aimed at schools to encourage better health behaviour:
www.wiredforhealth.gov.uk

If you want to know more about the medicines you have been prescribed go to:
www.rxlist.com

The authoritative source of drug information in the UK is the BNF which is updated regularly and used throughout the National Health Service:
www.bnf.org.uk

three

Pain

Introduction

Pain is part of everyday life. Although we try to avoid it or remove it, we can never be pain-free. If I walk into a door, it hurts. It's nature's way of saying, 'Don't walk into doors, fool!'.

IN THIS CHAPTER WE WILL LOOK AT:

- types and theories of pain
- measuring pain
- controlling and managing pain.

Types and theories of pain

THE PUZZLE OF PAIN

It seems obvious that pain is connected with injury. I touch a hot oven, I injure my hand, and it hurts. So, does our experience of pain occur as a consequence of damage to body tissue? The answer is both yes and no. The study of pain presents a number of puzzles that challenge the link between tissue damage and feelings of pain. These puzzles include the experience of injury with pain, the experience of pain without injury, and the poor relationship between the size of the injury and the size of the pain.

An example of injury without pain is **episodic analgesia,** where people do not feel pain for some minutes or hours after an injury. The type of injuries involved in episodic analgesia range from minor abrasions to broken bones or even limb loss. Episodic analgesia is a puzzle for any theory of pain. The tissue damage is surely greatest at the time of the injury but the pain is delayed. This experience seems to be quite common – Melzack *et al.* (1982) discovered that 37 per cent of people arriving at the accident and emergency department of an urban American hospital with a range of injuries reported the experience of episodic analgesia.

There are also a number of examples of pain where there is no obvious physical cause including neuralgia, causalgia, headache and phantom limb pain. **Neuralgia** is a sudden sharp pain along a nerve pathway. It occurs after a nerve damaging disease (for example, herpes) has ended. **Causalgia** is a burning pain that often develops as a consequence of a severe wound, for example from a knife. The remarkable thing about causalgia, like neuralgia, is that it develops after the wound has healed. Causalgia and neuralgia are not constant pains but they can be triggered by a simple stimulus in the environment, such as a breeze or the vibration of an air-conditioning unit.

Sometimes people who have lost a limb, or were born without a limb, experience all the sensations of having that limb. This experience is commonly referred to as **phantom limbs**, and they have been recorded for over a century. One of the striking features about these phantom limbs is that people can experience very real pain from their phantoms. This raises a number of questions about how we experience pain and, more generally, how our senses work, and how we interpret sensory information.

An early explanation was that the cut nerve ends, which grow into nodules called neuromas, continue to produce nerve impulses which the brain interprets as coming from the lost limb. Working on this hypothesis various cuts have been made in the nerve pathways from the neuromas to the brain in an attempt to remove pain. These cuts, like other surgical attempts to relieve pain, sometimes bring about short-term relief, but the pain usually returns after a few weeks, and the cuts do not remove the phantom. Other theories have looked at nervous system activity in the spinal cord and the brain. None of these approaches is able to account for all the phenomena associated with phantom limbs.

the purpose of pain

Nobody wants pain but without it we would have serious problems. Pain seems to have three useful functions:

1. It can occur before a serious injury develops; for example, picking up something hot and immediately dropping it because of the pain
2. It can aid learning and help people avoid harmful situations in the future
3. When it occurs in damaged joints and muscles, pain sets a limit on activity and this helps the person to recover and also to avoid further damage.

This is not the whole story, though, and some pains serve no useful purpose. In fact, far from being the sign of a problem, pain can become the problem itself. Pain can become so severe and so feared that people would prefer to die than continue living with it. All these observations leave us with more questions than answers, although psychologists have attempted to respond to the puzzle of pain by developing explanations and interventions that relieve the suffering of pain.

what is pain?

Pain can be defined as '… an unpleasant sensory and emotional experience associated with actual or potential tissue damage, or described in terms of such damage' (Merskey and Bogduk, 1994). It helps our understanding of pain to divide up the experience into four components (Loeser and Melzack, 1999):

- **nociception**: the detection of tissue damage by specialised nerves in the body. Anti-inflammatory drugs such as aspirin produce pain relief mainly by restoring the nociceptive nerves to their resting state.
- perception of pain: our sense of pain. This can be caused by injury but, as shown above, it can occur without it.
- suffering: a negative response brought on by pain, and also by fear, stress and loss. Not all suffering is caused by pain, but with our medical view of the world, we commonly describe suffering in the language of pain, and so sometimes mislead the doctor and patient about the cause of the suffering.
- pain behaviours: the things a person does or does not do that can be put down to pain. For example, saying 'ouch!', or grimacing or playing dead. We observe these behaviours and use them to make judgements about the existence of nociception, pain and suffering.

THEORIES OF PAIN

The traditional approach to pain was **specificity theory**, which basically proposed that a special system of nerves carries messages from pain receptors in the skin to a pain centre in the brain. One of the points in favour of this approach was the discovery that there are specialised receptors in the skin for different sensations like heat and touch. The problem with the approach, as Melzack and Wall (1988) point out, is that the specialised receptors respond to certain unpleasant stimuli (a physiological event), but this does not mean that we always feel pain (a psychological experience). The examples of injury without pain, described above, show that there is not a direct connection between stimulation and pain. This point is reinforced by the evidence from neuralgia and causalgia, where a gentle touch can trigger a painful reaction.

A further argument against specificity theory comes from physiological evidence. For example, the technique of **neurography** allows us to record the activity of specific nerves, and we can match this activity up to the sensations that people are feeling. This research found that there is not a close connection between the activity of certain nerves and particular sensations in the person. For example, Chery Croze and Duclaux (1980) found that the onset of pain was not connected with the onset of activity in the specialised nerves. Also, different painful stimuli such as chemicals, pressure and heat provoke activity in different groups of nerves, but people are unable to tell the difference between the different stimuli, despite getting these different messages in their nervous system.

pattern theories

Pattern theories, in contrast to specificity theories, suggest that there are no separate systems for perceiving pain, but instead the nerves are shared with other senses like touch. According to these theories, the most important feature of pain is the pattern of activity in the nervous system that is affected by a number of factors including the amount of stimulation. For example, as the pressure of touch increases, the sensation will develop into one of constriction and eventually one of pain.

It is very difficult to build up an accurate 'wiring diagram' of the nervous system and to identify all the active bits of it. There is however a general belief that there are three types of receptor cells and nerve pathways that are important in pain. First, there are nociceptive cells that respond to pain but not to other stimuli. Second, there is another class of cells that respond to intense

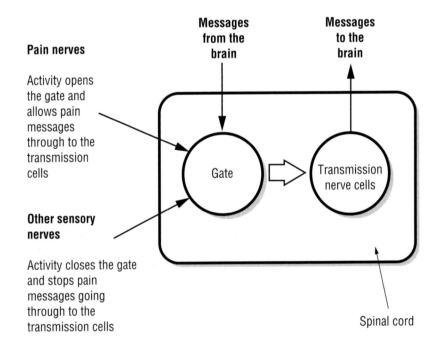

• **Figure 3.1:** The gate control theory of pain

stimuli (in other words, pain) as well as weak stimuli like touch. Third, there is a class of cells which respond just to touch and not to pain. So how do we make sense of all this nervous system information and feel pain? This brings us to the best current model of the phenomena – the gate control theory.

gate control theory

The **gate control theory**, first proposed by Melzack and Wall in the 1960s, combines the medical approach of previous theories with psychological and social factors that contribute to the experience of pain – the biopsychosocial approach. The theory suggests that there is a 'gate' in the nervous system that either allows pain messages to travel to the brain, or stops those messages (see Figure 3.1).

The gate control theory is biologically quite complex and the description of the nervous system pathways is beyond the scope of this text. The theory describes in some detail which nerves produce what reaction in the nervous system, and proposes a model for the control of the transmission of pain messages up the spinal cord to the brain. According to the theory, the gate is in the spinal cord and the factors that open or close it are:

1. *Activity in the pain fibres* – this is the 'specificity' part of the theory, and suggests that activity in the small diameter fibres, which respond specifically to pain, will open the gate.
2. *Activity in other sensory nerves* – this is the 'pattern' part of the theory and refers to the large diameter nerves that carry information about harmless sensations such as touching, rubbing or scratching. Activity in these nerves will close the gate – this goes along with the observation that light rubbing around painful areas will reduce the pain.
3. *Messages from the brain* – this is the central control mechanism and it responds to states such as anxiety or excitement to open or close the gate. The idea that the brain can influence the experience of pain explains why distracting people can help them not to notice the pain so much.

There are a number of factors that act to open or close the pain gate and a summary of these is shown in Figure 3.2 on p.60.

Points about the gate control theory:
- **Sensation** and **perception**: when we consider vision we recognise that we do not just respond to visual stimuli but actively create our image of the world. The gate control theory suggests that a similar process is operating in pain. We actively interpret the various sensations to arrive at our experience of pain.

Conditions that open the gate	Conditions that close the gate
Physical conditions	**Physical conditions**
● Extent of the injury	● Medication
● Inappropriate activity level	● Counterstimulation, e.g. massage
Emotional conditions	**Emotional conditions**
● Anxiety or worry	● Positive emotions
● Tension	● Relaxation
● Depression	● Rest
Mental conditions	**Mental conditions**
● Focusing on the pain	● Intense concentration or distraction
● Boredom	● Involvement and interest in life activities

• **Figure 3.2:** Conditions that can open or close the pain gate (Source: Sarafino, 1994)

- Causes of pain: the gate control theory suggests that pain is a combination of physical and psychological factors.
- The wiring diagram that is often presented with discussions of the gate control theory is a model based on the best available evidence. As yet, only some of the features of the model have been discovered in the nervous system, and so it remains a model that explains the evidence rather than an accurate description of nervous system pathways. The model does, however, have a lot of support and it is accepted as a useful model for discussion and research about pain.

beyond the gate control theory

The gate control theory did not take into account the long-term changes in the nervous system brought on by tissue damage and other external factors. Physiological and behavioural studies have shown that learning has a role to play in pain. It is clear that the brain can generate pain even without sensory input from nociceptors or the spinal cord – for example, phantom limb pain (Melzack, 1992). One explanation is to suggest that the brain has a way of creating an image of the body on which sensory data is played out. This is referred to as the **neuromatrix** (Loeser and Melzack, 1999). It is perhaps helpful to think of the neuromatrix as a hologram that the brain uses as a reference point for making sense of the array of sensory information it has to deal with. The hologram is the map and the sensory information colours it in. Needless to say, it is impossible to test for the existence of the neuromatrix.

FACTORS AFFECTING PAIN

There are a number of factors that have been found to affect the experience of pain including:

- *Learning*: for example, if you show migraine sufferers words associated with pain, it increases their anxiety and their sense of pain (Jamner and Tursky, 1987).
- *Anxiety*: for example, women with pelvic pain appear to show a correlation between anxiety and the strength of the pain (McGowan *et al.*, 1998).
- *Gender*: women have been shown to find post-surgical pain more intense than men, though men are more disturbed by low levels of pain that last several days (Morin *et al.*, 2000).
- *Cognition*: the way we think about the pain, whether we feel in control of it, or whether we feel able to do something about it, may well affect our sense of pain. This forms the basis for cognitive therapies described later in this chapter.

> Pain is a complex experience with a variety of physiological and psychological components. Although we have an understanding of some of the factors that increase or reduce pain, we do not yet have a complete picture of it.
>
> **Section summary**

Measuring pain

'This won't hurt a bit' says the doctor, just before inflicting excruciating pain on you by shoving a giant needle into your bottom. How does the doctor know how much pain you will feel? It is important that we are able to know *how much* pain people are feeling, and it is also important to know *what type* of pain they are feeling. Like most personal experiences, it is difficult to make comparisons between what I experience and what you experience, and so psychologists have a problem when they try to measure pain.

One approach to pain measurement is that of Karoly (1985) who suggests that we should not just focus on the immediate experience of pain but should examine all the factors that contribute to pain. Karoly identifies six key elements:

1. *Sensory* – for example, the intensity, duration, threshold, tolerance, location.
2. *Neurophysiological* – for example, brainwave activity, heart rate.
3. *Emotional and motivational* – for example, anxiety, anger, depression, resentment.
4. *Behavioural* – for example, avoidance of exercise, pain complaints.
5. *Impact on lifestyle* – for example, marital distress, changes in sexual behaviour.
6. *Information processing* – for example, problem-solving skills, coping styles, health beliefs.

The methods that psychologists can use to collect information about pain include interviews, psychometric measures, physiological measures, behavioural observation and medical records.

INTERVIEWS

The main advantage of the **interview method** is that it can be used to cover most of the elements suggested by Karoly (see p.61). The interview can collect information about the effect of pain on the lifestyle of the patient, the patterns of behaviour before and after the onset of the pain, and also information about family interactions, relationships, performance at work and exercise. The problem is the time taken to obtain the information and the skill required to interpret the responses.

Theme link to Methodology (**psychometric measurement**)

- Measuring people

To measure something you have to compare it against something else. If we are measuring a table, it is easy because we can use a ruler, but if we are measuring people what can we use? There are three ways in which we can use tests to measure people:

1. Direct measurement: where we use a physical measure such as grip strength or reaction time. Although these measures can be useful, there are only a limited number of direct measures we can make of people.
2. Criterion-referenced measurement: where we compare the performance of an individual against an ideal performance.
3. Norm-referenced measurement: where we compare the performance of an individual against the performance of other people, most commonly the peer group. This is far and away the most common way of using psychological tests.

- Test reliability

If we are using a psychometric test we need to know whether it will give us a consistent result. So if we give someone the test on a Wednesday afternoon, we hope to get the same results as if we had given the test on a Friday morning. It would be remarkable if we got exactly the same result, because all forms of measurement have an element of error in them, but we hope this error will be relatively small.

> • Test validity
> A test is said to be valid if it measures what it claims to measure. So we need to consider whether a pain scale measures pain, and whether an IQ test measures intelligence. This is not as obvious as it sounds, and it can be a complex process to measure validity. In the measurement of pain the various scales often give quite different results (Zalon, 1999). The question arises as to whether they are measuring different types of pain (and are therefore all valid measures), or whether only some of the recognised pain scales can be considered to be valid.

QUESTIONNAIRES AND RATING SCALES (PSYCHOMETRIC MEASURES)

The more common way of obtaining information about pain is to use questionnaires and rating scales such as the McGill Pain Questionnaire (Melzack, 1975). This questionnaire, shown in Figure 3.3 on p.64, has questions that refer to sensory elements of pain, emotional elements, evaluative (cognitive) elements and miscellaneous elements.

The MPQ has been extensively used and extensively researched. It is seen as being generally reliable and valid (Karoly, 1985) but it is not without some criticism. There are some questions about how well it can distinguish between different types of pain, and it is also possible to criticise it for the language it uses and the different ways that different people will interpret it.

A variation of this was developed by Varni et al. (1987) for use with children (see Figure 3.4, p.65). This illustrates the problems that we face when we are trying to measure experience, and that is the different language that different groups of people use. Children do not use adult descriptions of their experience so we are dependent on the observations of their parents and any other inventive ways we can develop to probe their thoughts and feelings.

PHYSICAL MEASURES

One of the early areas of study in psychology was **psychophysics**, where an attempt was made to describe sensation in the same terms that we describe things in physics. In the area of pain there have been attempts to measure the *pain threshold* (the smallest amount of a stimulus required to create the experience of the pain), and also the unit of *just noticeable difference* (JND). The JND is the smallest change in the stimulus (such as heat) that produces an experience of *greater* pain. These two measures have not been found to be very useful in a clinical setting (Wolff, 1980), but useful information has come from the measurement of *pain tolerance*, the *drug request point*, and the *pain sensitivity range*, which is the difference between the pain threshold and the pain tolerance point.

Part 1.   **Where is your pain?**

Please mark, on the drawing below, the areas where you feel pain. Put E if external, or I if internal, near the areas which you mark. Put EI if both external and internal.

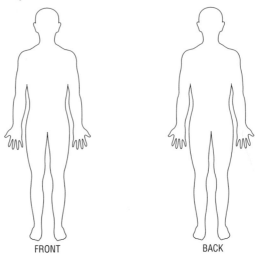

FRONT   BACK

Part 2.   **What does your pain feel like?**

Some of the words below describe your *present* pain. Circle *ONLY* those words that best describe it. Leave out any category that is not suitable. Use only a single word in each appropriate category – the one that applies best.

1	2	3	4
Flickering	Jumping	Pricking	Sharp
Quivering	Flashing	Boring	Cutting
Pulsing	Shooting	Drilling	Lacerating
Throbbing		Stabbing	
Beating		Lancinating	
Pounding			
5	**6**	**7**	**8**
Pinching	Tugging	Hot	Tingling
Pressing	Pulling	Burning	Itchy
Gnawing	Wrenching	Scalding	Smarting
Cramping		Searing	Stinging
Crushing			
9	**10**	**11**	**12**
Dull	Tender	Tiring	Sickening
Sore	Taut	Exhausting	Suffocating
Hurting	Rasping		
Aching	Splitting		
Heavy			
13	**14**	**15**	**16**
Fearful	Punishing	Wretched	Annoying
Frightful	Gruelling	Blinding	Troublesome
Terrifying	Cruel		Miserable
	Vicious		Intense
	Killing		Unbearable
17	**18**	**19**	**20**
Spreading	Tight	Cool	Nagging
Radiating	Numb	Cold	Nauseating
Penetrating	Drawing	Freezing	Agonizing
Piercing	Squeezing		Dreadful
	Tearing		Torturing

• **Figure 3.3:** Extract from The McGill Pain Questionnaire

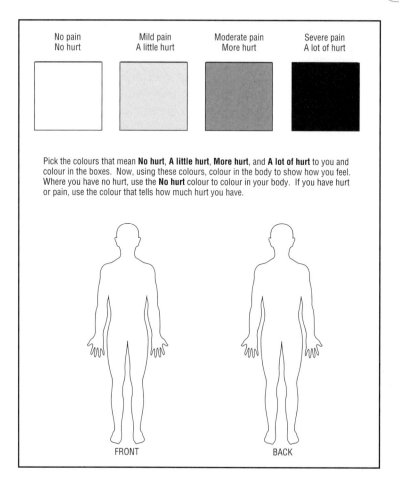

| No pain | Mild pain | Moderate pain | Severe pain |
| No hurt | A little hurt | More hurt | A lot of hurt |

Pick the colours that mean **No hurt, A little hurt, More hurt,** and **A lot of hurt** to you and colour in the boxes. Now, using these colours, colour in the body to show how you feel. Where you have no hurt, use the **No hurt** colour to colour in your body. If you have hurt or pain, use the colour that tells how much hurt you have.

FRONT   BACK

• **Figure 3.4:** Extract from the Varni-Thompson Paediatric Pain Questionnaire

It is perhaps not surprising, given the complex nature of pain already described, that physiological measures are unreliable. For example, attempts to measure joint inflammation by thermography or muscle tension by electromyogram (EMG) have not been helpful in assessing pain. Likewise, measures of skin temperature, blood flow and skin resistance have produced inconsistent findings in studies of headaches (Horn and Munafò, 1997). Even studies of the neurotransmitters associated with pain (for example, beta-endorphin) have not consistently found a relationship between the level of the chemical and the level of pain (Bernstein *et al.*, 1995).

MEASURING PAIN BEHAVIOUR

Pain behaviour includes all the different ways to communicate pain, such as complaints, gestures and postures, etc. It also includes the numerous ways, both adaptive and maladaptive, that we use to cope with pain, such as relaxation or behaviour to avoid the onset of a painful episode. One of the common methods of measuring these behaviours is to ask the patient to fill in a pain behaviour diary, which covers things such as sitting position, walking position, use of medication, and general movement during the day. Another method is to use a standard observation framework, such as the UAB Pain Behaviour Scale (Richards *et al.*, 1982) which can be administered and scored quite quickly by health professionals. This scale asks the observer to rate such things as mobility, facial grimaces and the amount of time spent lying down.

Section summary   As with all attempts to measure behaviour and experience, pain poses a number of problems, including the need to rely on the self-reports of people with pain. They, in turn, have to make comparative judgements about their pain without ever knowing what pain is like for other people.

Controlling and managing pain

There are numerous ways to alleviate pain and it is not possible in this text to do more than provide some examples from the range of different methods. We will look at some chemical treatments, surgical attempts, physical therapies, electrotherapies and psychological treatments.

CHEMICAL TREATMENTS

A clergyman from Chipping Norton (yes, it does exist) wrote to The Royal Society in 1763, to describe how useful the extract of willow was in the relief of rheumatism and bouts of fever. The active ingredient of willow extract is acetylsalicylic acid which we are more familiar with as *aspirin*. Aspirin, and other similar drugs such as ibuprofen, have three therapeutic actions: first against pain, second against inflammation and third against fever. They appear to work on the damaged tissue that is causing the pain and inflammation, and they have no known effect on the nervous system. These drugs are heavily used today and the only drawback is the number of side-effects, such as gastric irritation and bleeding and also (with large doses) deafness. There is another mild **analgesic** called acetaminophen (more commonly know as *paracetamol*) which has similar pain relief properties to aspirin. It does not, however, have the same anti-inflammatory action as aspirin and it is not known how it creates analgesia.

Another major set of chemicals used in pain relief come from the opium poppy and are referred to as **opiates**. The medical value of the extract of this poppy has been known for thousands of years and its use is recorded as far back as 1550 BC. A number of chemicals have been made from this poppy including morphine, heroin and codeine. Although the different chemicals vary in the amount of pain relief they produce they all produce analgesia and, as the dose increases, also produce drowsiness, changes of mood and mental clouding. Opiates act on the central nervous system in the brain and also in the spinal cord. Their most likely action is to inhibit pain messages from travelling to the brain – in other words, they close the gate. The main reason that opiates are so effective in pain control is that the nervous system contains many nerves that respond to chemicals that are very similar to opiates. These nerves are involved in the experience of pain, though their action is complex and not yet fully understood.

We usually take drugs by injection or by swallowing pills, though if you are very unlucky you might receive the medication by suppository. However, a development in pain control has been to allow patients to self-administer the drug by pressing a button on a small machine beside the bed. The machine is set up so that the patient cannot accidentally (or on purpose) give themselves too much medication. Patients do not take this opportunity to give themselves the largest possible amount of medication, but use their control over the drug to balance the pain with the mental clouding that high doses produce. The technique was originally used on adults but is now commonly used with children as young as five years with pain from surgery, burns or cancer (MacDonald and Cooper, 2001). Studies on children with severe pain following spinal fusion however have found that it is not enough just to give control of pain relief to the patient. It is also necessary to use non-drug therapies to produce consistent relief from severe pain (Kotzer and Foster, 2000).

placebos

Placebos are treatments with no obvious active ingredients that bring about relief of symptoms. This is a controversial area because of the interpretations of the effects of placebos. For example, if someone reports a reduction in pain after taking a non-active drug, does this mean the pain was 'all in their head'? There is also the further problem of the ethics of placebo trials. For example, a number of sham operations were carried out on people suffering from angina pain (Diamond, 1960). Half the patients were given a real heart bypass operation, and half were given an operation without the bypass. The study suggested that both groups had equal reduction in pain, indicating that the operation procedures alone were enough to reduce angina pain. The question is whether you would be happy to go into a placebo group if you had a heart condition.

Theme link to Methodology (**experimenter effect**)

Painkillers may work better if you believe in them, and they may also work better if the doctor believes in them. In a study on pain placebos (Gracely *et al.*, 1985) patients were given one of three medications: (a) an analgesic (painkiller), (b) a placebo, or (c) naloxone (which blocks the action of pain-relieving nerves and may therefore increase pain). The patients were therefore told to expect less pain, no change or more pain. The doctors who gave them the drugs were also put into two groups: (a) those who believed that the patients might receive a painkiller, and (b) those who believed that the patients had no chance of receiving a painkiller. This sounds confusing, but the aim was to see whether the doctor's beliefs would have an effect on the effectiveness of a placebo.

All the patients were, in fact, given placebos. The results showed that if the doctors believed that the patient may have received a painkiller, then the patient reported pain reduction, but if the doctor believed that patient had no chance of receiving a painkiller, there was no such pain reduction. This is an example of the **experimenter effect** (described by Rosenthal and Fode, 1963) where the results recorded are in line with the expectations of the experimenter.

SURGICAL ATTEMPTS

Medical people have attempted to reduce pain through surgery by cutting nerve pathways or making lesions in special centres in the brain. One condition that has attracted surgery is *trigeminal neuralgia* which produces persistent and excruciating pain in the face. When medication fails to deal with the pain, surgeons will destroy the branch of sensory nerves to the facial area. This produces numbness in the face, but sadly only gives temporary relief from the pain which recurs in many patients. This is the same story as other surgical interventions, in that any pain relief that occurs is usually only temporary. This only goes to show how complex our pain senses are. On the whole, surgical techniques are only recommended for people with terminal illnesses who want medium-term relief from pain to make the rest of their lives more comfortable.

PHYSICAL THERAPIES

There are a wide range of physical therapies that are used to relieve and control pain. These include: *manual therapies* such as massage, *mechanical therapies* such as traction, *heat treatments* such as microwave diathermy and ultrasound, *cold treatments* such as ice packs, and *acupuncture.*

Heat is widely used in the treatment of pain and is reported to be most effective for deep tissue injuries such as bruises, torn muscles and arthritis. It is not known whether it speeds up the repair of these injuries, but the general belief is that this is doubtful. It seems quite remarkable, given the extensive use of this treatment, that we do not know how it works. One hypothesis for the action of this treatment and many other physical treatments is that they produce sensory inputs that end up inhibiting the pain signals (they close the gate).

Acupuncture is the ancient art of sticking needles into people. There has been considerable scepticism in the West about this Eastern treatment, but it is now accepted as a treatment for pain, and there are examples of its successful use on people with chronic pain. In a study on hospice patients where weekly acupuncture treatments were given over a six-week period, patients reported an excellent or good response to the acupuncture in over 60 per cent of the cases, and the majority of patients had no adverse effects (Leng, 1999). Also, a review of acupuncture use for recurrent headaches found that it had some use, although the quality of evidence was not fully convincing (Melchart et al., 1999). Other review studies have also found this mixed evidence for the effectiveness of the treatment. Some studies on chronic pain found acupuncture provided some relief, but again the evidence was not convincing (Smith et al., 2000, Ezzo et al., 2000). The problem with the evidence is the lack of controlled trials which compare acupuncture with sham acupuncture – placebo controls where you presumably stick needles in anywhere rather than in the acupoints. Although acupuncture often seems effective compared with no treatment at all, it does not do so well when compared with placebos.

electrotherapies

The practice of using electrical stimulation for pain control is centuries old. Recent techniques apply the stimulation to the spinal cord, parts of the brain, peripheral nerves and traditional acupuncture points (White et al., 2001). *Spinal cord stimulation* (SCS) is used to treat a wide variety of inoperable and chronic pains, but it is invasive and expensive and only tends to be used when most other treatments have failed. *Deep brain stimulation* has been used for about 50 years and involves inserting electrodes into the brain. As with SCS it is only used when other less dangerous or invasive methods have failed. One method that has attracted a lot of research is *transcutaneous electrical nerve stimulation* (TENS). (Note: *transcutaneous* means through the skin). In this treatment, the patient receives mild pulses of electricity in the painful area through gel pads attached to the skin. It has been found to reduce chronic pain in a wide variety of conditions including neuralgia and arthritis. TENS has recently been used with women in labour, and van der Spank (2000) reported 96 per cent satisfaction with the treatment and significantly less pain during the birth. *Percutaneous electrical nerve stimulation* (PENS) is similar to TENS but instead of gel pads, the stimulation is administered via acupuncture-like needles inserted under the skin.

Clearly there are enough electrotherapies around to cause a meltdown of the National Grid, but there are still some doubts about them because it is not clear how they work. As a result they usually come under the heading of 'complementary therapy'.

PSYCHOLOGICAL TREATMENTS OF PAIN

As we have seen in the previous sections of this chapter, psychological factors play a big role in the experience of pain. Over the past few years there has been a growing acceptance of the value of psychological interventions in the treatment of pain. Included in these interventions are relaxation, biofeedback, hypnosis, cognitive coping skills, operant techniques, mental imaging, self-efficacy and counselling.

operant techniques

The idea behind **operant techniques** is to use the principles of operant conditioning to encourage behaviours that reduce pain and discourage behaviours that increase pain. Erskine and Williams (1989) suggest that these methods work by:

- using social reinforcement and periods of rest to gradually increase activity levels
- gradually decreasing the use of medication
- training people associated with the patient (medical staff and family) not to reinforce the pain behaviours through their sympathy and practical help.

This approach only deals with behavioural responses to pain and is most useful if someone has actually developed inappropriate behaviours for dealing with their pain, such as the excessive use of drugs or the avoidance of activity. However, if someone has chronic pain from cancer, for example, then this approach is likely to have only minor value.

coping training

Basler and Rehfisch (1990) looked at how **coping** training could be used to help people who were suffering from chronic pain. They developed a twelve-week intervention package, which included training patients to reinterpret the pain experience, training in physical relaxation techniques, avoiding negative and catastrophic thinking, and training in how to use distraction at key times. They found that compared with an untreated waiting list control group, there were significant improvements for these patients at a six-month follow-up. The patients reported fewer general and pain-related symptoms, and a lower level of anxiety and depression. There was also a decline in the number of visits they made to the doctor.

The implication of the study is that behavioural interventions to enhance coping skills in distressing medical conditions can be beneficial and relatively long-lasting. There are, of course, always problems with this type of study. For example, it is always possible that the patients were responding to the additional interest in their cases shown by those who had developed the training strategy; without the introduction of a third group who received just as much attention, it is not possible to be sure that this has not happened. (Although many of those working with chronic pain patients would argue that even if there was this type of 'placebo effect' going on, it wouldn't matter – the important thing is that the patients subjectively experienced less pain as a result of what happened to them!)

cognitive behaviour therapy (cbt)

Cognitive behaviour therapy makes two assumptions (Turk and Fernandez, 1991). First, that our thoughts (cognitions), feelings, behaviour and motivation are all connected to each other, and second that people are adaptive and continually make judgements about their situation and their capacity to deal with it. Turk and Fernandez suggest there are three ways that CBT can be used to alleviate cancer pain:

* changing maladaptive behaviours
* changing self-statements, images and feelings that interfere with everyday life
* changing assumptions and beliefs that bring about unhelpful thoughts about yourself (for example, 'I am helpless') and the pain (for example, 'it can't be controlled').

CBT was used with patients recruited from seven London hospitals who had sickle cell disease pain. Their progress was measured using a variety of psychometric measures, including the General Health Questionnaire (GHQ) and the Pain Self-Efficacy Questionnaire (PSEQ). CBT was shown to be effective for the patients immediately after the treatment and also at a two-month follow-up. It was able to reduce the psychological distress, reduce the pain and improve the level of coping (Thomas *et al.*, 1999).

Although we only have a sketchy understanding about the causes of pain, there are a wide range of treatments to relieve it. These treatments include physiological, physical, cognitive and behavioural treatments which often work best when used in combination.

Section summary

KEY TERMS

analgesic
causalgia
cognitive behaviour therapy
coping
episodic analgesia
experimenter effect
gate control theory
interview method
neuralgia
neurography
nociception
operant technique
opiate
pain
pattern theory
perception
phantom limbs
placebo
psychophysics
sensation
specificity theory

EXERCISE 1

Try to describe two different types of pain, for example toothache
and indigestion. You might use the McGill Pain Inventory to help
you find the right words. What makes these pains feel worse and
what makes them feel better?

EXERCISE 2

Try to imagine a world without pain (I wonder if you can), and think
what problems it would present for you.

(a) Describe what psychologists have found out about what pain is and how we can measure it.

(b) Discuss the psychological evidence on pain and its measurement.

(c) Suggest one psychological technique that could be used to reduce the distress of chronic back pain. Give reasons for your answer.

Further reading

The classic book to read on pain is Melzack, R. and Wall, P. (1988) *The challenge of pain*. London: Penguin.

If you are interested in the phenomenon of pain then you will be interested in Melzack, R. (1992) Phantom limbs, *Scientific American*.

Websites

The Pain Society is the representative body for all professionals involved in the management and understanding of pain in the United Kingdom. The Pain Society aims to achieve the highest possible standards in the management of pain, through education, training and research in all fields of pain, and by facilitating the exchange of information and experience: www.painsociety.org/

The American Pain Society can be found at: www.ampainsoc.org/

four

Stress

Introduction

Stress – who needs it? Well, the strange answer is that we probably all do.
We seek it out as much as we avoid it. Nearly everyone could have an easier
life if they didn't work so hard, play so hard, do so much or think so much.
So, what is this feeling of stress and why do we have it?

IN THIS CHAPTER WE WILL LOOK AT:

- causes and sources of stress
- measures of stress
- management of stress.

Causes and sources of stress

One of the first things to do is to define our terms. As ever in psychology, this
is not an easy task, but it is helpful to think of the **stress experience** as being
made up of two major components: stressors and the stress response.
Stressors are stimuli that require a person to make some form of adaptation
or adjustment. These stressors usually bring out a relatively stereotyped set of
biological and psychological responses – the **stress response**.

Stressors can be *external*, for example, environmental changes such as
heat, crowding, or noise. They can also be social events such as difficulties
with a loved one, or contact with a hated one. These are events that happen
outside of yourself but have a stressful effect. On the other hand, stressors
can also be *internal* (inside yourself), for example pain can create a stress
response, as can your thoughts and your feelings.

The relationship between stressors, the stress response and our
experience of stress is not straightforward. We might suggest that heat is a
stressor that will bring out a stress response and make us feel under stress.

However, for those of you who have ever chased the sun on your holidays, you will know that heat, a beach and a cool drink are blissfully relaxing. So, the effect of stressors is affected by the situation we are in and the sense we make of what is happening. The position is further complicated by the fact that some stressors can be viewed as positive, for example, many people seek out big crowds to enhance their sense of excitement. Also, there are large individual differences in our responses to stressors: one person might dissolve into a puddle of tears when they miss a train, whereas another person might shrug their shoulders and have a beer while they wait for the next one.

All this means that it will not be simple to define and measure stressors. Likewise, the stress response is quite complex and is made up of numerous physiological, cognitive, affective and behavioural components.

The early work on stress looked mainly at biological responses in the person and so adopted the **biomedical model** (see the Introduction to this text). The responses that created the most interest were *arousal* (the functions of the autonomic nervous system), the *flight or fight response*, and the *general adaptation syndrome* (Selye, 1973). More recently psychology has taken a very different approach, looking at the interaction between these biological responses and the psychological changes within a person and also the social context in which they are living (the biopsychosocial model).

STRESS AND ILLNESS

The scientific argument goes as follows: A situation that is threatening to an individual brings about a response in the hypothalamus (a brain structure), which prepares the body for action by bringing about changes in the autonomic nervous system, the neuroendocrine system and the immune system. These changes provide energy for muscles, reduce non-essential activity such as digestion, and prepare the **immune system** to deal with wounds efficiently. This is a very useful set of changes for any animal in a threatening situation where a physical response is the best option, and it probably evolved under the pressures of evolution. The problem comes in modern life where we often have stressful experiences to which physical response is either prohibited or not appropriate. In this case the biological changes are not useful, and if they are maintained over a long time they may have a harmful effect (Willemsen and Lloyd, 2001).

Our understanding about the body's response to threat has led psychologists to consider how stress contributes to the development of illness. A review of recent findings (Senior, 2001) highlighted a number of connections between stress and ill health, for example:
- caregivers of relatives with dementia had lower than average levels of immunity to pneumonia, which suggests that severe and chronic stress can have an effect on the immune system.

- depression has been found to play a role in the development of heart disease and also breast cancer, and depression has also been shown to have a measurable effect on the immune system.

All of this raises many questions, such as which comes first, the changes in the immune system or the feelings of stress? Perhaps the stress is a *response* to the illness rather than a *cause*. With regard to breast cancer, there have been many studies carried out on the relationship between psychological factors and development of the disease. A review of 48 such studies found only a modest association between the factors. This challenged the popular belief that personality and stress influence the development of breast cancer (McKenna *et al.*, 1999).

We should also remember that, as well as having an effect through physiological changes, stress can influence disease by affecting our behaviour and perception. Under stress we might increase our unhealthy behaviours, such as drinking alcohol and smoking, and we might decrease healthy behaviours like sleeping well and taking exercise. We might also have a different view of the world and perceive ourselves as having less control or as being less able to do anything about our situation. Clearly the relationship between stress and illness is complex and involves physiological, behavioural and psychological components.

MODELS OF STRESS

Sarafino (1994) defines **stress** as:

> ... the condition that results when the person/environment transaction lead the individual to perceive a discrepancy – whether real or not – between the demands of a situation and the resources of the person's biological, psychological and social systems. (p.74)

This definition looks beyond the biological changes and includes the social and psychological changes as well. One of the key features of this approach is to look at the gap between what we think *we have to* do to deal with a situation and what we think *we are able to* do. This gap depends on how we appraise a situation and how we appraise ourselves. Lazarus and Folkman (1984) suggest that we make two cognitive appraisals: first, whether the stressor or event poses a threat (the primary appraisal), and second, whether we will be able to cope with it (the secondary appraisal) (see Figure 4.1).

COGNITIVE APPRAISAL

In the primary **appraisal** we judge whether the event is *positive, negative* or *neutral*. So, developing a cold one evening might be positive (because you won't have to go to work tomorrow), it might be neutral (because you are able

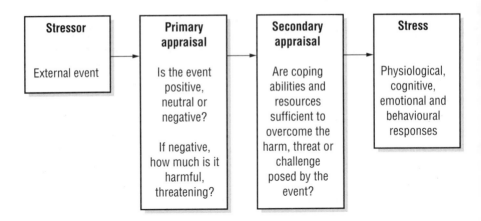

• **Figure 4.1:** The experience of stress

to carry on with whatever you intended to do whether you have a cold or not), or it might be stressful (because you have an examination or interview tomorrow and you think you will not be able to do your best).

If we judge that the event is negative then we make further judgements on three issues. First, how much *harm* has already occurred ('oh no, it's already a nightmare!'), second, what is the *threat* of further harm ('tomorrow will be a disaster!'), and third, what sort of *challenge* does this event offer ('I'll boldly go where no-one has gone before!').

In the secondary appraisal we have to make judgements about our own abilities and our current state of mind and health. It doesn't necessarily follow on after the primary appraisal and it sometimes might even affect the primary appraisal, so if you make the assessment that you are in a poor state of mind (secondary appraisal of coping ability), this might lead you to see a normally safe event as being quite threatening (primary appraisal). For example, if you don't feel able to cope with people today, then a visit to the newsagent for the *News of the World* could appear quite taxing!

PERSONAL QUALITIES AFFECTING APPRAISAL OF STRESS

Our appraisal of stress can be affected by our personal qualities, our personal circumstances, and also by the type of event that is causing the stress. Among the personal qualities that psychologists have studied include how hardy we are. Kobasa (1979) suggested that we can identify personality characteristics that separate out people who get ill under stress and people who remain healthy. She called the collection of these characteristics **hardiness**.

Hardiness is made up of three components – *control, commitment* and *challenge*. Control refers to the belief that a person can influence events in their life (see the section on locus of control in Chapter 7), commitment refers to a person's sense of purpose or involvement in their life, and challenge refers to the tendency to see problems as an opportunity for personal growth.

Support for the connection between hardiness and health came from a study by Kobasa (1979) who looked at the health of executives in a large American corporation. She used a questionnaire to divide the executives into two groups, one who had experienced a high level of stress and a high level of illness, and one who had experienced a high level of stress but without much illness. When she assessed the hardiness of all the executives she found that the low illness group appeared to be hardier than the high illness group.

Although this approach is quite appealing there are a number of problems with it. First, the many attempts within psychology to identify personality all run into difficulties because of the complex and changing nature of an individual's personality. It does not seem to be possible to find one characteristic that affects all of their behaviour, and perhaps it is not very useful to try to do this. Second, much of the work on hardiness was carried out on groups of workers and it is not clear whether this is a useful concept for looking at illness. Most commonly it is still used with work groups alongside the idea of burnout ('I can't take it any more'). For example, Sciacchitano *et al.* (2001) investigated radiographers in hospitals and found that hardiness had a beneficial effect in reducing the impact of stress and reducing the chances of burnout.

CULTURE AND STRESS: JOHN HENRYISM

There is some American research that helps our understanding of the health of ethnic minority groups. A study on hypertension found that black men living in high stress environments (high unemployment, high crime, low incomes) had higher blood pressure than those living in low stress environments (James *et al.*, 1987). This relationship between environmental stress and blood pressure was not found in white men. James *et al.* suggested that the high blood pressure was a response to an active coping style used by some black men who tried to change their environment. He developed a psychometric scale to measure this active coping style and named it the John Henry Scale, after a legendary black worker who had battled against the odds to win a physical contest but then dropped dead from physical and mental fatigue. James found that black men who scored high on his scale of **John Henryism** were three times more likely to have hypertension.

The coping strategy that is measured in the John Henryism scale concerns gaining control over your life and changing your circumstances. For many people this is a sign of good health, and for the white men in the study, a high score on the John Henryism scale did not coincide with hypertension. The black men with the high score, in fact, tended to be satisfied with their lives and perceived their own health to be good. James suggests that the attempt to heroically change your circumstances when you have very little power to make any real difference can have a damaging effect on your health. This makes an interesting addition to the discussion about locus of control (see Chapter 7).

The effect is strongest in poor black communities, and has not been found in, for example, black college students (Jackson and Adams-Campbell, 1994). Further studies have found that black college students with high levels of support from family and friends reported lower levels of stress than those without social support, and that raised blood pressure was related to high scores on tests of **hostility** (Adams et al., 1999). Also, the effect of John Henryism on blood pressure is dependent on gender. Men and women face different cultural expectations and social pressures in their communities. A study of 600 adults in the African-American community of a town in southern USA found the expected relationship between John Henryism and blood pressure in men, but the effect was reversed in women (Dressler et al., 1998). Clearly to understand this condition we need to explore the relationships between the physiological variables (blood pressure), the psychological variables (John Henryism) and the social variables (class and gender).

Section summary   Stress can be analysed in terms of stressors and the stress response. An important component in our experience of stress is the way we interpret stressors and our ability to deal with them. Sources of stress are quite varied and people react to them in individual ways.

Measures of stress

One of the most important contributions that psychology can make is the development of measuring techniques. If we want to investigate stress and develop stress reduction techniques then we need to have some way of measuring how much stress people are experiencing. If we continue with the division of the stress experience into stressors and the stress response then we can look at measures for these in turn.

MEASURING STRESSORS

There have been numerous attempts to measure how stressful particular events are, including the following three areas:

1. Measuring the effects of stressors by looking at performance on simple behavioural tasks, or by using self-report scales (asking people to rate how stressful an event was)
2. Stressful life events (see below)
3. Social environment or social climate: Moos (1973) suggested that social environments, like people, have unique 'personalities' – some are supportive and others are more controlling. All environments will have physiological, psychological and behavioural effects on the people interacting with it. Moos and Moos (1981) looked at a number of social climates – including psychiatric wards, college dormitories, prisons, work groups, families – and described the general characteristics of the environments. Research has suggested that positive environments will enhance normal development and reduce recovery time from illness, but responsibility, work pressure and change can increase the likelihood of illness or subjective distress.

STRESSFUL LIFE EVENTS

The starting point for most discussions on **stressful life events** is the Social Readjustment Rating Scale developed by Holmes and Rahe (1967). They looked at what events and experiences affect our level of stress, and they developed a scale to measure this. The scale looks at the stress caused by major life events (the sort of events that we experience as difficult to deal with) and is based on previous research which found that some social events that required a change in lifestyle were associated with the onset of illness. They developed the scale by asking nearly 400 adults to rate 43 different life events for the amount of adjustment needed to deal with them. From their responses they developed the Social Readjustment Rating Scale which is shown in Table 4.1.

The researchers compared the responses of the different groups of people within their sample and found a startling degree of agreement. They compared the responses of different age groups, men and women, Catholics and Protestants, and in all cases found very high correlations in their ratings of stressful events. The one exception was the correlation of the responses of black participants with white participants which, although still quite high, was much lower than the other correlations.

To measure your personal stress score with the Social Readjustment Rating Scale, tick off the events that have occurred to you in a given time, usually 12 months or 24 months, and add up the readjustment values. According to Holmes and Rahe, the higher the number you end up with, the

• **Table 4.1:** The Social Readjustment Rating Scale. Source: Holmes and Rahe (1967)

Rank	Life event	Mean value
1	Death of spouse	100
2	Divorce	73
3	Marital separation	65
4	Jail term	63
5	Death of close family member	63
6	Personal injury or illness	53
7	Marriage	50
8	Fired at work	47
9	Marital reconciliation	45
10	Retirement	45
11	Change in health of family member	44
12	Pregnancy	40
13	Sex difficulties	39
14	Gain of new family member	39
15	Business readjustment	39
16	Change in financial state	38
17	Death of close friend	37
18	Change to different line of work	36
19	Change in number of arguments with spouse	35
20	Mortgage over $10,000	31
21	Foreclosure of mortgage or loan	30
22	Change in responsibilities at work	29
23	Son or daughter leaving home	29
24	Trouble with in-laws	29
25	Outstanding personal achievement	28
26	Wife begins or stops work	26
27	Begin or end school	26
28	Change in living conditions	25
29	Revision of personal habits	24
30	Trouble with boss	23
31	Change in work hours or conditions	20
32	Change in residence	20
33	Change in schools	20
34	Change in recreation	19
35	Change in church activities	19
36	Change in social activities	18
37	Mortgage or loan less than $10,000	17
38	Change in sleeping habits	16
39	Change in number of family get-togethers	15
40	Change in eating habits	15
41	Vacation	13
42	Christmas	12
43	Minor violations of the law	11

more chance you have of developing an illness. A number of studies, by Holmes and Rahe in particular, have shown a connection between high ratings and subsequent illness and accident, though according to Sarafino (1994) the correlation between rating and illness is really quite weak (r = 0.3).

There are a number of problems with this method of measuring stress, and before reading on you might like to look at the scale – what criticism would you make of it as an attempt to measure stressful life events?

problems with the social readjustment rating scale

- major life events are quite rare and many people will score near to zero
- some of the items in the scale are vague or ambiguous
- some of the items will have greater value for some groups in society than others
- there are large individual differences in our ability to cope with stressful events
- there are large cultural and sub-cultural differences in our experience of events
- the value of events changes with time and changing social customs.

It is worth noting, however, that the measurement of psychological phenomena is a singularly difficult enterprise, and it is usually easier to come up with criticisms of existing systems than to devise better ways of doing things.

The stressful life event approach to stress and illness generated a considerable amount of research, not least because the Social Readjustment Rating Scale developed by Holmes and Rahe provides a relatively straightforward way of measuring stress. It also conforms to everyday notions of the effect of dramatic events in our lives. In accounts of personal experience recorded in news reports it is not unknown for people say how a particular event, such as unexpected bereavement, or desertion by a loved one, has 'shattered my life'. But Kanner et al. (1981) argue that the minor stressors and pleasures of everyday life might have a more significant effect on health than the big, traumatic events assessed by the Holmes and Rahe scale, particularly in view of the cumulative nature of stress.

Kanner et al. (1981) developed a scale to explore these small events, which they called the **Hassles and Uplifts** Scale (see Table 4.2). They administered the checklist to 100 middle-aged adults once a month for ten months. The Hassles scale was found to be a better predictor of psychological problems than life event scores, both at the time and later. Scores on the Uplift scale, however, only seemed to relate to symptoms in women. The men in the study seemed relatively unaffected by uplifts.

• **Table 4.2:** The Hassles and Uplifts Scale for middle-aged adults. Source: Kanner *et al.* (1981)

Ten most frequently expressed hassles of middle-aged adults

1   Concerns about weight
2   Health of a family member
3   Rising prices of common goods
4   Home maintenance
5   Too many things to do
6   Misplacing or losing things
7   Outside home maintenance
8   Property, investment or taxes
9   Crime
10   Physical appearance

Life events and hassles and uplifts measures continue to be used in health research and produce mixed results about the effects of these stressors. For example, a study of 73 adults with psoriasis (a serious skin condition) compared their stressful life events scores with patients with skin conditions other than psoriasis. The strongest predictor of developing the disorder was a family history of it in parents or siblings. The study also found evidence that stressful life events are a predictor of the disease (Naldi *et al.*, 2001). In contrast, a study of over 400 people aged 32 or 33 looked for a connection between stressful life events, uplifts and hassles, and the biological risk factors for coronary heart disease (CHD). Although the uplifts were found to be related to positive lifestyles, no relationship was found to the key biological risk factors for CHD (Twisk *et al.*, 2000).

MEASURING THE STRESS RESPONSE

The attempts to measure various aspects of our responses to stress include *biochemical* measures, *behavioural observation,* and *cognitive* measures.

Biochemical research has looked at the effects of stress on various processes in the body, such as those associated with adrenaline, noradrenaline and also the immune system. **Behavioural observation** has included work on specific behaviours, such as facial expressions, rate of speech, posture and nail-biting. It has also included a number of self-report measures on topics as diverse as marital satisfaction and frequency of urination. **Cognitive measures** have looked at the perceived control someone experiences over their life, their perceived level of arousal (often different to the actual level of physiological arousal), and their mood and attitudes.

In health psychology, there have been a number of stress measures developed to investigate the response to illness, injuries, and medical treatments. An example of this approach is the Perceived Stress Scale (Cohen *et al.*, 1983) which asks people to rate 14 items on a five-point scale for frequency of feeling stress during the previous month. For example, one of the items is 'In the last month, how often did you have to deal with irritating life hassles?' Another commonly used scale is the General Health Questionnaire (GHQ) (Goldberg, 1978), and this gives a measure of psychiatric disorder.

Theme link to Methodology (**demand characteristics**)

In any situation we try to make sense of things and behave appropriately, as the situation demands. Therefore any attempts to measure people's behaviour are likely to have some demand characteristics, where the research inadvertently cues the participant to respond in a particular way (Orne, 1962).

One of the issues with stress scales is that they commonly find that people have stress, which you could argue is like finding that the sky is blue. Sometimes people are cued into giving stress responses. A review of stress in UK doctors (McManus *et al.*, 1999) challenged previous findings which showed doctors to have higher levels of stress than other professional groups and higher than the general population. The measure of stress used was the GHQ which (when used correctly) does not include stress but only mentions 'medical complaints' and 'health in general'. In the initial studies of doctors, the GHQ was sent out as a measure of stress and work problems. When the GHQ was used in the correct context by McManus *et al.*, the levels of stress recorded by the doctors were equivalent to those in the general population. The demand characteristic here is clearly to reply that you are stressed. Imagine being in a job and telling people that you are on top of everything and feel relaxed. If you do this, everyone will think you do not have enough work to do. There is a demand characteristic that we should be working under pressure and report feeling stressed.

A general problem with self-report measures such as these is that they ask for simple responses from people and so are unable to capture the richness and variety of human experience. The alternative is to use interviewing techniques and sophisticated coding of people's responses. One of the best known measures in this field is the Life Events and Difficulties Schedule (LEDS) (Brown and Harris, 1989). This schedule looks at a range of issues to do with health, employment, social roles, etc. but requires trained interviewers and trained judges to operate it.

OTHER METHODS OF MEASURING STRESS

There have been numerous attempts to measure stress and the items described above just give a flavour of this effort. Each measure has its limits but they all provide some clues to the experience we have of stress. One of the problems with many stress measures is that they make just one recording (a snapshot) of the stress level. However, the experience of stress is very variable throughout the day, and also from day to day. In order to understand the pattern of changes in stress, psychologists have tried a number of techniques such as diary methods, where people record their responses to stress over a period of time. For example, Gulian *et al.* (1990) carried out a study of the pattern of stress in British drivers. The drivers completed a number of psychometric tests (for example, Rotter's Internal–External Locus of Control Scale) and filled in a diary of their feelings while driving over five days. They found that drivers experienced more stress in the evening and midweek. They also found that daily driving stress varied with age and experience, as well as with health condition, sleep quality, and driving conditions. It was also affected by the driver's overall perception of driving as a stressful activity.

Sometimes psychologists try to combine a variety of methods to obtain a clearer picture of stress. An example of this is a study by Douglas *et al.* (1988) who used a diary method and physiological measures to look at stress in fire-fighters. They studied a stratified sample of 100 fire-fighters from 12 different fire stations. The heart rhythm of each fire-fighter was recorded with a portable electrocardiogram for at least 48 hours while they were at work, and the results were analysed to give a 'ventricular cardiac strain score'. They were also asked to keep a diary during these stressful events. Higher scores were found in those under stress due to the number of call-outs, their level of seniority, and the stressful events they recorded in their diaries.

Section summary Stress is mainly measured through self-report which requires the individual to compare themselves against previous states of mind or their beliefs about other people's state of mind. Psychologists have developed a range of stress measures which are widely used in research on health.

Management of stress

There have been an amazing number of techniques developed to help people reduce their stress or to help them develop their coping skills. They use a variety of psychological concepts and theories, and although they each seem to have their uses, there is not a single easy answer to the stresses and strains of everyday living. The following section gives a flavour of the range of these techniques.

BIOFEEDBACK

The principle behind **biofeedback** is that we gain control over bodily functions and actions if we are aware of what is happening. However with most bodily reactions, such as our blood pressure, we are relatively unaware of what is happening and so are unable to control them. Biofeedback aims to give an individual some direct feedback about bodily responses and so encourage them to take control of that response. Biofeedback concentrates on biological systems that are not under conscious control but are having an adverse affect on the person.

The sort of information that can be given to a person includes the pattern of their brain activity (using an electroencephalogram), their heart rate, their skin conductance (using a galvanic skin response), and their temperature. An example of the application of biofeedback in health was developed by Budzynski, Stoyva and Adler (1970) who used the technique with tension headaches. Budzynski *et al.* gave their patients biofeedback of the muscle tension in their foreheads. They combined this biofeedback with training in deep muscle relaxation, and were able to provide relief for people with a long history of chronic headaches.

This seems to be a simple solution to the problem of headaches, but sadly nothing is ever that straightforward. The causes of headaches are far from clear, and there are numerous other factors apart from muscle tension that affect the onset and development of headaches.

IMAGERY

Techniques for training people to use mental **imagery** have proved helpful in stress reduction. Bridge *et al.* (1988) described how imagery was used to help to reduce the unpleasant emotional consequences of radiotherapy for women with breast cancer. In the study, women who were undertaking this treatment were allocated to one of three groups. Two of the groups were relaxation training groups: the first one just emphasised physical training, particularly control of muscle tension and breathing, while the second used relaxation training along with mental imagery, asking each person to concentrate on a peaceful scene of her own choice. The third was a control group. The control group were encouraged to meet and simply talk about themselves for the same amount of time as the two treatment groups.

Bridge *et al.* assessed the women's moods using standard psychometric tests, and found that women in both of the treatment groups were significantly less disturbed than those in the control group. However, it was also clear that those women who had been encouraged to use imagery techniques as well as relaxation were more relaxed than those whose intervention had focused only on physical relaxation. This appears to show the benefits of imagery, although it is not at all clear why or how imagery is effective.

RATIONAL EMOTIVE THERAPY

Since the experience of stress is affected by the way we cognitively appraise the situation, it follows that we can deal with stress through adjusting that appraisal. This is usually referred to as cognitive restructuring and one of the best known examples of this is **rational emotive therapy** (RET) which was developed by Albert Ellis (Dryden, 1996). According to Ellis, stress often comes from faulty or irrational ways of thinking. For example, *awfulising* is thinking that it is *awful* if you get reprimanded at work and *can't-stand-itis* is thinking that you *can't stand* being late for a meeting.

The therapy examines a person's thought processes and tries to change those thoughts and beliefs which are irrational and negative. The basic plan for RET is the A-B-C-D-E framework shown in Table 4.3 opposite. There is mixed reaction to the therapy, in particular whether people have any long-term change in their experience of stress.

STRESS INOCULATION

Some medical treatments give people weak versions of a disease in order to encourage the body to develop defences against the full-blown version. This is called inoculation. A form of cognitive therapy uses a similar idea as a preparation for a stressful event and it is called, not surprisingly, **stress-inoculation**. It was developed by Meichenbaum (1977) and it is designed to prepare people for stress and to help them develop skills to cope with that stress. The inoculation programme involves three stages:

1. *Conceptualisation* – the trainer talks with the patient about their stress responses, and during this phase the patient learns to identify and express feelings and fears. The patient is also educated in lay terms about stress and the effect it can have.
2. *Skill acquisition and rehearsal* – the patient learns some basic behavioural and cognitive skills that will be useful for coping with stressful situations. For example, they might be taught how to relax and use self-regulatory skills. The patient then practices these new skills under supervision.

• **Table 4.3:** The A-B-C-D-E framework for rational emotive therapy

A	is the ACTIVATING experience that creates the stress, for example being told by your partner that you are fat lazy loser who has no friends because you prefer to sit in at night and watch *Match of the Day*.
B	refers to the thoughts and BELIEFS that go through your mind in response to A. The thoughts might be quite reasonable such as 'I should go out more often', or unnecessarily negative such as 'I am a lazy useless loser and I should get a life'.
C	refers to the CONSEQUENCES of A and B. These might be quite positive like resolving to be more sociable and less tied to the television, or they might be quite inappropriate like feeling useless and even more socially inept than you really are.
D	refers to DISPUTING the irrational beliefs that forms part of the therapeutic approach and helps the person distinguish between true ideas such as 'I could behave better' and irrational ideas like 'I am a total loser'.
E	refers to the EFFECT of the therapy, which will hopefully consist of a restructured system of beliefs so that you can sit in and watch *Match of the Day* on a Saturday night without any guilt or feelings of uselessness.

[NOTE: I wouldn't want the reader to think that this is any way autobiographical]

3. *Application and follow through* – the trainer guides the patient through a series of progressively more threatening situations. The patient is given a wide range of possible stressors to prepare them for real life situations.

As with RET, the jury seems to be out on whether this is an effective intervention or not, though it has been used in sports with some effect to reduce stress. For example, Zeigler *et al.*'s (1982) study of cross-country runners showed that stress inoculation was useful in reducing stress and improving performance. It has also been widely used in workplaces: a review of 37 studies looking at the behaviour of 1,800 people suggested that the technique was useful in reducing performance anxiety, reducing general anxiety and enhancing performance under stress (Saunders *et al.*, 1996).

Section summary There are a range of techniques at our disposal to help people deal with stress and become better at coping. However, it must be said that sometimes stress is there for a reason, and it should not necessarily be coped with. Imagine a stressful work situation where people have unrealistic work schedules and are given little or no support. Should they be given stress counselling or should they be encouraged to take up trade union activity to negotiate for a better working environment? Psychologists are unfortunately drawn toward the counselling answer because they tend to concentrate on the individual and ignore the social and political world in which that person is living.

KEY TERMS

appraisal
behavioural observation
biofeedback
biomedical model
cognitive measures
demand characteristics
hardiness
hassles and uplifts
hostility
imagery
immune system
John Henryism
rational emotive therapy
stress
stress experience
stress response
stressful life events
stress-inoculation
stressors

Design your own hassles and uplifts scale. Make a list of the little
things in life that cheer you up, and those that irritate you. For
example, a sunny day (uplift), being cut up in traffic (hassle), getting
a call from someone you like (uplift), dropping your choc-ice
(hassle). When you have finished your list, use it for a few days and
see if the balance of uplifts and hassles matches your overall
experience of stress for the day.

Imagine a world without stress. What would have to change in
order to reduce your stress levels? Why don't you do this anyway?
Would the changes definitely make you happy?

ESSAY QUESTION

(a) Describe what psychologists have found out about stress and
how it can be managed.

(b) Discuss the psychological evidence on stress and its
management.

(c) Suggest one psychological technique for measuring stress in
people revising for their A levels. Give reasons for your answer.

Further reading

There are so many books written on stress that a whole rainforest full of paper
has been used. In fact, I've been kept awake worrying about the
environmental damage of all these stress books. If you want to investigate
this issue further then one of the best academic collections is Monat, A.
and Lazarus, R. (1991) *Stress and Coping*. New York: Columbia.

If you are interested in the practical attempts to deal with stress then have a
look at Hodgkinson, P.E. and Stewart, M. (1991) *Coping with catastrophe:
a handbook of disaster management*. London: Routledge.

Websites

There is so much material about stress on the web that it is hard to know where to start, and much of it is appealing to you to buy their book or stress reduction programme. The stress magazine at Channel 4 has some interesting material, and if you want to find out more about rational emotive behaviour therapy then go to the Albert Ellis site:

www.channel4.com/health/magazine/stress/

www.rebt.org/

same way as we can be addicted to alcohol? Yes we can, says a psychological approach to addictive behaviours such as that put forward by Orford (2001). He suggests the following definition:

> Addiction: an attachment to an appetitive activity, so strong that a person finds it difficult to moderate the activity despite the fact that it is causing harm (p. 18).

This approach suggests that people can develop addictive behaviours for a wide range of activities including drug-use, alcohol-use, gambling, game-playing, eating and sex. Although these behaviours appear to be very different, they involve a number of similar components. Griffiths (1995) suggests that addictive behaviours have six components:

SALIENCE: this refers to how important the behaviour becomes to the individual. The addictive behaviour becomes the *most* important activity for a person so that even when they are not doing it, they are thinking about it.

EUPHORIA: this is the experience people report when carrying out their addictive behaviour. People with addictive behaviour patterns commonly report a 'rush', a 'buzz' or a 'high' when they are taking their drugs or when they are gambling, for example.

TOLERANCE: this refers to the increasing amount of activity that is required to achieve the same effect. A drug addict might have to increase their intake of drugs and a gambler might have to increase the stakes.

WITHDRAWAL SYMPTOMS: these are the unpleasant feelings and physical effects which occur when the addictive behaviour is suddenly discontinued or reduced. This can include 'the shakes', moodiness and irritability. These symptoms are commonly believed to be a response to the removal of the chemical that the person has developed a tolerance to. However, they can also be experienced by gamblers (see Orford, 1985), so the effects might be due to withdrawal from the behaviour as well as the substance.

CONFLICT: people with addictive behaviours often develop conflicts with the people around them, often causing great social misery, and also develop conflicts within themselves.

RELAPSE: although people sometimes manage to shake off their addictive behaviour, the chances of relapse are very high. Even when the person has been 'dry' for a considerable time, they can quickly revert to the same high levels of addictive behaviour.

This psychological approach to addictive behaviours highlights the many similarities within a wide range of damaging behaviour patterns, and indicates that the disease model of addiction is quite limited.

Further similarities between a number of addictive behaviours can be found in the groups that support people who want to change their behaviour, such as Alcoholics Anonymous, Gamblers Anonymous, and even Weightwatchers. Orford (1985) suggests that when people change their addictive behaviour it might involve them reinventing themselves, which means they take on a new identity and change their attitudes and values on a wide range of issues. The organisations that support this change often have a religious approach to the problem. They frequently require the person to give a personal testimony ('I was a sinner', 'I was a drunk', 'I was a gambler') and accept the authority of the group or a 'higher power'. They usually emphasise that the person should change from being self-centred (egocentric) and pleasure-seeking (hedonistic), to being humble and ascetic. All this suggests that the person is undertaking a moral (or spiritual) change rather than a medical change. Perhaps it is not surprising then that the expert treatments offered by psychologists and health workers have only a small role to play in helping people change their appetitive behaviour.

Section summary   Addiction and substance abuse are difficult to define. A medical approach tends to see these behaviours as a disease, whereas a psychological approach might well see them as extreme examples of everyday behaviour. The behaviours can also be seen as lapses in moral strength.

Theories of substance use and abuse

BIOLOGICAL EXPLANATIONS OF ADDICTIVE BEHAVIOUR

The medical approach to addiction looks for biological explanations of these behaviours. One of the key questions is: why do people do something that appears to be harmful to their health? What is the reward they get from it?

Biological explanations of addiction focus on neurotransmitter substances in the brain, and on genetic differences between people with addictions and people without addictions.

Theme link (**Reinforcement**)

Reinforcement is anything that increases the probability that a behaviour will recur in similar circumstances. The term commonly refers to learned associations, acquired through operant or classical conditioning, but it may also be applied to other forms of learning.

A possible answer to the question of what makes something reinforcing comes from the discovery of 'pleasure centres' in the brain. Olds and Milner (1954) found that rats would press a lever for the reward of mild electrical stimulation in particular areas of the brain. The rats would continue to press the lever in preference to other possible rewards such as food, drink or sexual activity. The researchers did not record whether the animals had silly smiles on their faces, but these areas of the brain are now commonly referred to as 'pleasure centres'.

The experience of pleasure is very important for our healthy development. If, for example, we found food or sex boring, then our species would starve to death or fail to breed. The feelings of pleasure associated with these activities act as a reinforcement. If we associate these pleasure feelings with other activities, then they too will be reinforced. So, the pleasure that encourages essential behaviours is also the pleasure that can encourage damaging behaviour. Could it be that the threat of addiction is the price we pay for pleasure?

neurotransmitters

Without going into a full biology lesson, a **neurotransmitter** is a chemical which moves in the gaps between nerve cells to transmit messages. If the chemical is blocked or replaced, for example, then the message changes and there is an effect on the physiological systems, and also on cognition, mood and behaviour. The neurotransmitter that is most commonly implicated in all this is dopamine, but a range of other chemicals have also been found to have an effect (Potenza, 2001).

The difficulty with looking at which neurotransmitter produces which reward is that – to state the blindingly obvious – the brain is remarkably complex, and the effects of even one drug can be very diverse. Ashton and Golding (1989) suggest that nicotine can simultaneously affect a number of systems including learning and memory, the control of pain, and the relief of anxiety. In fact, it is generally believed that smoking nicotine can increase arousal and reduce stress – two responses which ought to be incompatible (Parrott, 1998). This means that it is difficult to pin down a single response that follows smoking a cigarette. A deeper problem with the neurochemical explanations is that they can neglect the *social* context of the behaviours. The pleasures and escapes associated with taking a drug are highly varied and depend on the person, the dose, the situation and the wider social context in which they live (Orford, 2001).

genetics

Until relatively recently the main way of investigating **genetic** factors in human behaviour was to study family relationships. More recently it has been possible to carry out genetic analysis and look for differences in the genetic structure of people with and without addictive behaviours. The two methods tend to point to different answers. The family studies emphasise the role of *environmental* factors in the development of addictive behaviours. A study of over 300 monozygotic twins (identical) and just under 200 same-sex dizygotic twins (fraternal) estimated the contribution of genetic factors and environmental factors to substance use in adolescence. It concluded that the major influences on the decision to use substances were environmental rather than genetic (Han *et al.*, 1999). Some family studies, however, suggest there is a link between addictive behaviour and personality traits. For example, a study of over 300 monozygotic twins and over 300 dizygotic twins looked at the relationship between alcohol use and personality. The study suggests that there is a connection between genetics and anti-social personality characteristics (including attention-seeking, not following social norms, and violence), and between these personality characteristics and alcoholism (Jang *et al.*, 2000).

Studies that analyse the genetic structure of individuals tend to emphasis the role of *genetics* (rather than the environment) in addictive behaviours. Some genes have attracted particular attention and have been shown to appear more frequently in people with addictive behaviours than in people without. The problem is that these genes do not occur in all people with the addictive behaviour and they do appear in some people without it. For example, a gene referred to as DRD2 (no, he didn't appear in Star Wars) has been found in 42 per cent of people with alcoholism. It has also been found in 45 per cent of people with Tourette's syndrome and 55 per cent of people with autism. It has also been found in 25 per cent of the general population. This means that DRD2 appears more frequently in people with these behavioural syndromes, but it can not be the sole explanation for the behaviour (Comings, 1998).

Theme link (**Nature and nurture**)

The **nature-nurture** debate in psychology swirls around how much behaviour or cognition or emotions are determined by our genetics' (nature), or by our experiences in life (nurture).

Both nature and nurture clearly have an influence. Without a body and brain we cannot exist and without care and attention we cannot survive. So the argument might appear to be pointless, but the relative importance of the two factors will have an influence on how we deal with a variety of issues. If, for example, alcoholism is something people are born with, then there is little point in having treatment to help them change their lives. The best treatment might even be to prevent alcoholics from having children and therefore passing on the disease. See how tricky it all gets?

availability

There are a number of environmental factors that affect the incidence of addictive behaviours in a society. Two factors which affect the level of alcoholism are the *availability* of alcohol, and the *average consumption* of alcohol by the general population. Comparison studies have found near perfect correlations between the number of deaths through liver cirrhosis (generally attributed to alcohol abuse) and the average consumption of alcohol in different countries (for a discussion see Orford, 1985). The availability factor also affects the consumption of cigarettes, as shown in the study below.

If we examine the pattern of cigarette consumption compared with the retail price of cigarettes in the UK we can observe a remarkable relationship. Figure 5.2 shows how the curve for consumption is the mirror image of the curve for retail price (Townsend, 1993). Since 1970 any increase in price has brought about a decrease in smoking. At the time of the study there was a slight decrease in the price of cigarettes (figures adjusted to take account of inflation) and a corresponding rise in smoking. This rise in smoking was particularly noticeable in young people and, according to Townsend (1993), regular smoking by 15-year-old boys increased from 20 per cent to 25 per cent and by 16–19-year-old girls from 28 per cent to 32 per cent. This connection between price and consumption suggests an obvious policy for governments who want to reduce smoking.

social cues: tobacco advertising

In their response to the Health of the Nation strategy (DoH, 1992), the British Psychological Society (1993) called for a ban on the advertising of all tobacco products. This call was backed up by the government's own research (DoH,

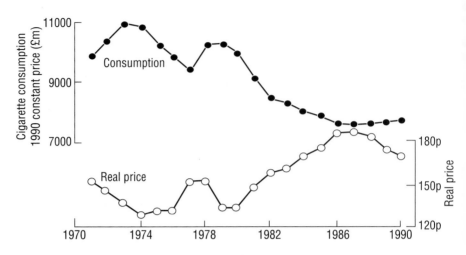

• **Figure 5.2:** The relationship between the price of cigarettes and consumption 1971–1990

1993) which suggested a relationship between advertising and sales. Also, in four countries that have banned tobacco advertising (New Zealand, Canada, Finland and Norway) there has been a significant drop in consumption.

Public policy, however, is not always driven by research findings, and the powerful commercial lobby for tobacco has considerable influence. In her reply to the British Psychological Society, the Secretary of State for Health (at that time Virginia Bottomley) rejected an advertising ban, saying that the evidence was unclear on this issue and that efforts should be concentrated elsewhere. This debate highlights how issues of addictive behaviours cannot be discussed just within the context of health. There are a range of political, economic, social and moral contexts to consider as well. At the time of writing, both the British government and the European Community have now made commitments to ban tobacco advertising in the near future.

the spiral model of behavioural change

People sometimes give up addictive behaviours after seeking professional help, and they sometimes give up these behaviours through their own efforts. When people manage to change themselves without professional help it may be referred to as 'spontaneous remission'. This is a patronising description that implies the change just happened to the person and required no effort or decision from them. It also implies that the only meaningful change in behaviour is one that is brought about through professional guidance. Prochaska, DiClemente and Norcross (1992) looked at both professionally initiated and self-motivated changes in behaviour to see if there were any common features. Their paper 'In Search of How People Change' reviews the evidence and puts forward a five-stage **model of behavioural change**.

The five stages are:

PRECONTEMPLATION: in this stage, the person has no intention of changing their behaviour and probably does not even perceive that they have a problem. The problem might be obvious to the person's family and friends, but the person might well respond to these concerns by saying 'I know I have some faults but there is nothing I really need to change'.

CONTEMPLATION: in this stage, the person is aware that they have a problem and they are thinking that they should do something about it. However, they have not yet made a commitment to take action. People can stay in this stage indefinitely, and Prochaska *et al.* quote some of their own research that observed some smokers who were stuck in the contemplation stage for the full two years of the study.

PREPARATION: in this stage, the person is intending to take action in the near future and may well have already started to do something. Most commonly they will have reduced the number of cigarettes they smoke, or delayed the time of the first cigarette each day. If this was a race then people in this stage are at the 'get set' point, just before they start to run.

ACTION: in this stage, people change their behaviour, or their experience, or their environment, so that they can overcome their problem. A person is said to be in the action stage if they have successfully altered their behaviour for a period of between one day and six months. In the case of smoking the change must involve not smoking at all. People often incorrectly see the action stage as the main part of change and overlook the importance of the preliminary stages that prepare the person for change, and the efforts that are required to maintain the change.

MAINTENANCE: in this stage, the person works to prevent a relapse and to consolidate the changes they have made. Someone is said to be in the maintenance stage if they are able to remain free from the problem behaviour for more than six months.

The model shown in Figure 5.3 presents change as a spiral. This takes account of the observation that most people who take action to change a habit are not successful at the first attempt. Prochaska *et al.* (1992) suggest that smokers commonly make three or four action attempts before they reach the maintenance stage.

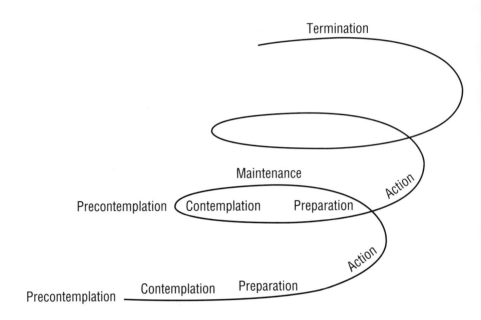

• **Figure 5.3:** The spiral model of change proposed by Prochaska, DiClemente and Norcross (1992)

Section summary   There are a number of factors that are believed to have an effect on addictive behaviours, including neurotransmitters, genetics, environmental and social influences. The jury is still out on the relative importance of these factors.

Preventing and quitting

REINFORCEMENT

One way to reduce substance abuse is to give people rewards for not taking the substance. There are two psychological ways of looking at this: one is to see it as *reinforcement* for a behaviour, and the other is to see it as a *distracter* from the pleasurable reinforcement of the substance. A programme in the US, reported by Mestel and Concar (1994), tried to change the behaviour of people with a serious cocaine problem. The subjects of the programme had their urine tested several times a week for traces of cocaine, and every time it was clear of any cocaine they were given vouchers. The vouchers started with a value of $2.50, but every time they were clear of cocaine the value went up by $1.50, so that if they had ten consecutive clear tests they would receive $17.50 for the next clear test. If they had one test that showed traces of cocaine then the payments went back to $2.50 again.

The best way to cash in on this programme, then, was to stay clear of cocaine for as long as possible.

The vouchers were backed up with counselling on how best to spend the money, so they were encouraged to spend it on, for example, sports equipment to take up a hobby, or a family meal in a restaurant to help build up relationships which might have been damaged by the substance use. This voucher-therapy approach was reported to have good results. The norm for drug treatment programmes is a drop-out rate of 70 per cent within six weeks. On this programme, however, around 85 per cent stayed in the programme for twelve weeks and around two-thirds stayed in for six months.

The problem with this approach is not its success rate, but the reaction of other people to the idea of giving drug users money not to take drugs. It is not difficult to imagine the hostile reaction of politicians and the general public to this sort of programme. It is the same hostile reaction that is met by harm minimisation programmes which seek to reduce the dangers to health in people carrying out risky behaviours.

HARM MINIMISATION

Health education programmes that encourage people to stop taking drugs are remarkable unsuccessful. The message 'Hey kids, just say 'No!" does not produce much reduction in substance use. An alternative approach is to encourage **harm minimisation**. These controversial campaigns accept that people will engage in risky behaviour and try to reduce the health risks by encouraging users to take the drug safely. One way of reducing the health risks for intravenous drug users is to provide needle exchanges so that they do not share injecting equipment. Using sterile equipment dramatically reduces the risk of getting blood infections such as hepatitis or HIV and AIDS.

Safer drug use can be encouraged by messages for harm minimisation which involve a hierarchy of behavioural changes such as:

- do not use drugs
- if you must use drugs, do not inject
- if you must inject, do not share equipment
- if you must share, sterilise the injecting equipment before each injection.

The harm minimisation programmes also give information on how to sterilise injecting equipment easily and effectively (see the example in Figure 5.4). Instead of treating drug dependency by trying to achieve abstinence, this approach tries to educate drug users about safe practices they can adopt to minimise the risks to themselves and others. Another way of reducing the potential harm to intravenous drug users is to provide medically controlled drugs as a substitute for street drugs. These drugs, such as methadone, are less harmful than street heroin, partly because they are free from impurities.

• **Figure 5.4:** Example of a harm minimisation programme for intravenous drug users. An eight-foot tall 'Bleachman' distributes packets of bleach to intravenous drug users on the streets of San Francisco. An extensive advertising campaign backs up the scheme with instructions for users on how to sterilize their needles with bleach. The move is to counter the growing threat of HIV/AIDS among intravenous drug users who acquire the virus through sharing infected needles

Harm minimisation programmes can improve the health of drug users, but they attract a lot of criticism because they appear to condone drug use.

The public resistance to the above approaches for dealing with excessive drug use suggest that concerns about personal health are not the only ones we have to take into account when designing health programmes. It appears that health workers have to take account of the moral concerns of their society as well as the health needs of their clients.

changing cognitions and changing behaviour

Dijkstra and De Vries (2001) investigated the extent to which self-help interventions change specific cognitions, and the extent to which changes in these cognitions are related to behaviour. They carried out a field experiment with follow-ups after 2 weeks and 12 weeks. Over 1,500 smokers were randomly assigned to one of four conditions offering self-help materials to aid giving up smoking. The research used two types of information: (a) information about the outcomes of smoking such as shorter life expectancy and various unpleasant diseases, and (b) **self-efficacy** information telling people how to be successful at giving up. The four groups were given the information as follows:

- group 1: just given information about the outcome of continuing to smoke
- group 2: just given self-efficacy enhancing information
- group 3: given outcome and self-efficacy information
- group 4: given no information.

The response rate of the smokers was 81 per cent after 2 weeks and 71 per cent after 12 weeks, which is pretty good for this sort of study. Table 5.1 shows the proportion of people after 12 weeks who had not smoked for the previous 7 days (7 days quit) and the number of people who had attempted to quit during the previous 12 weeks (quit attempt).

• **Table 5.1:** Proportion of people reporting smoking behaviour after 12 weeks (data in percentages)

	7 days quit	quit attempt
group 1	4.8	25.5
group 2	8.5	27.3
group 3	8.1	24.6
group 4	3.2	15.6

The table shows that about a quarter of the smokers had attempted to quit but most had started smoking again. This might be a bad thing because it gives them an experience of failure and hence lowers self-efficacy, but it might well be a learning experience that helps them to be successful in the future. The main conclusion from the study is that self-efficacy information seems to be effective, whereas the outcome information had no significant effect. We now go on to look at a number of other methods used to help people quit smoking.

nicotine substitution

There are various ways of allowing people to get their dose of nicotine without the dangerous activity of smoking. The idea behind nicotine substitution is that smokers will be able to change their habits of smoking without suffering the cravings associated with nicotine withdrawal. However, if we follow the model of addictive behaviours proposed by Griffiths (described above) then we might expect some smokers to have withdrawals from the habits of smoking as much as they would from the nicotine itself. Methods of substituting nicotine include nasal droplets (a bit embarrassing to use in public), chewing gum, and skin plasters (patches). All of these methods have been useful in helping some smokers though, as in all treatments, the relapse rate is quite high.

exercise

There have been a number of attempts to help people give up smoking by encouraging them to take regular exercise. A review of these studies, however, found that very few of them provided clear evidence for a positive effect of this approach (Ussher *et al.*, 2000). Among the problems with studies like these is the issue of measuring the addictive behaviour. If the study is following the disease model then it will probably see smoking in absolute terms of yes/no, rather than the number of cigarettes smoked. Therefore it is less likely to get successful results because if someone reduces their smoking but still has the occasional crafty smoke then they will be classified as a smoker.

skills training

Programmes have been developed in **coping skills**, such as reminding people of the negative consequences of smoking and positive consequences of quitting, *social skills*, such as helping people reject cigarettes that are offered to them and *relaxation skills*, such as learning alternative ways to deal with stress.

other behavioural methods

The behavioural method of **aversive conditioning** attempts to associate smoking with unpleasant sensations. One way of doing this is by rapid smoking. The smoker is asked to inhale deeply and frequently (every 6 seconds instead of the average 90 seconds) until they begin to feel ill and stop. The smoker eventually starts to associate smoking with feeling sick, and so becomes averse to cigarettes. An alternative method based on **operant conditioning** requires the smoker to pledge money to an organisation they dislike and make them pay up if they start to smoke again. The idea behind this method is that a person will find the thought of giving money to such an organisation so unpleasant that they will feel it is not worth starting to smoke again.

IS GIVING UP A NATURAL PROCESS?

Some people argue that giving up is a natural consequence of developing a strong or excessive appetite (Orford, 2001). This argument points out that expert treatments only have a limited success, and that the success occurs regardless of the treatment that is used. Treatments that are very different in intensity or in theory have a similar beneficial effect. Orford concludes that there is a lot of evidence that people give up excessive appetites (or addictions) without the help of experts. Perhaps psychologists should take more account of the lay view of addiction that it is a problem of 'weakness of will' as Heather (1994) suggests.

Section summary

There are more treatments for giving up alcohol, smoking and the rest, than you can wave a hypodermic at. Many individuals are able to use these treatments to bring about a desired change in their behaviour. There is no particular treatment or theory that appears to offer the definitive answer to the problems of addictive behaviours. The puzzle is why people cannot stop doing behaviours that damage their health. It can't be that difficult can it? Don't go to the shop, don't buy the cigarettes, don't open the packet, don't put one in your mouth, and don't set fire to it. You only have to achieve one of these to kick the habit. If only it was that simple.

KEY TERMS

addiction
addictive behaviour
aversive conditioning
coping skills
genetic
harm minimisation
model of behavioural change
nature–nurture
neurotransmitter
operant conditioning
opiates
psychoactive
reinforcement
self-efficacy
substance
substance dependence

EXERCISE 1

It is tricky finding activities on this topic that are safe and legal. You might try looking at the ingredients list on your food to see how many psychoactive drugs you are consuming each day. For example, look for caffeine.

EXERCISE 2

Imagine you are a heavy smoker or drinker and identify the benefits of giving up (for example, saving money) and the costs (for example, pain and discomfort).

ESSAY QUESTION

(a) Describe what psychologists have found out about the use and abuse of substances.

(b) Discuss the psychological evidence on substance use and abuse.

(c) Suggest one technique to prevent people starting the use of a substance. Give reasons for your choice.

Further reading

If you can get access to an academic library then you might like to read Orford, J. (2000) Addition as excessive appetite. *Addiction*, 96, 15–31. Alternatively you could pick up Heather, N. and Robertson, D. (1989) *Problem drinking*. Oxford: Oxford University Press.

Websites

There are loads of sites on drugs, smoking and alcohol. Some are self-help sites, some are commercial sites, and some offer information. You might try Alcoholics Anonymous or QUIT which are organisations dedicated to encouraging people to give up alcohol or tobacco:
www.alcoholicsanonymous.org
www.quit.org.uk

DrugScope is a UK-based drugs charity and centre of expertise on drugs. It provides balanced and up-to-date drug information to professionals and the public, conducts research and develops policies on drugs and drug-related issues. It also promotes humane and effective ways of responding to drugs and drug use, encourages informed debate and provides a voice for over 800 member bodies working on the ground: www.drugscope.org.uk/home.asp

You could also try the website of the American National Institute on Drug Abuse:
www.nida.nih.gov/

Health promotion

Introduction

What is health promotion? There is a growing awareness that there is more to health promotion than telling people to wrap up on a winter's day and eat their greens. Our health is affected by environmental, social, and political factors as well as the more obvious biological ones.

IN THIS CHAPTER WE WILL LOOK AT:

- methods of promoting health
- health promotion in schools, worksites and communities
- key issues in health promotion.

Methods for promoting health

One of the famous stories of early health promotion concerns the Broad Street pump in Soho, London. In 1854, Dr. John Snow plotted cases of cholera on a map of London and noticed that they clustered around a water pump on Broad Street (see Figure 6.1). At that time, water in London was provided by a number of private companies, and Snow discovered that the death rate from cholera was much higher for people using water from two of these companies (71 deaths per 10,000 people) than the others (only 5 deaths per 10,000 people). Snow's observation of the pattern of cases around Soho allowed him to carry out a natural experiment. He disabled the Broad Street pump by removing the handle (hi-tech or what?) and the cholera epidemic subsided in the area. From this, Snow was able to show that cholera was carried in water (Donaldson and Donaldson, 2000). As with all good stories, this one has probably grown a bit in the telling, and there is some suggestion that the epidemic was already declining before Snow disabled the water pump (McLeod, 2000), but the core of the story still holds some truths about health promotion.

• **Figure 6.1:** *On the mode of communication of cholera, area around Broad Street pump.* Snow's map of Soho with the black units showing the deaths from cholera between 19th August and 30th September 1854.

If we are going to improve the health of the nation it is important to consider what are the basic requirements for healthy living. The Ottawa Charter for Health Promotion (WHO, 1986) identified the following features that it believed were necessary for good health:

- peace
- shelter
- education
- food
- income
- a stable ecosystem
- sustainable resources
- social justice
- equity.

These features go far beyond the popular view of health promotion, and offer an ideal standard for our society to aim at. The current strategy of the British government is to promote health by developing three-way partnerships between individuals, communities and the government (DoH, 1999). The goals of this strategy are:

- to improve the health of the population as a whole by increasing the length of people's lives and increasing the number of years people spend free of illness
- to improve the health of the worst-off in society and narrow the health gap.

Health promotion activities

The activities of health promotion can be divided up into three overlapping areas, prevention, health education and health protection (Tannahill, 1985) as shown in Figure 6.2. The next brief section looks at some issues around prevention, and the rest of the chapter examines attempts to promote healthy living through education and through encouraging protective behaviour. Other chapters in this text also look at attempts to change behaviour, especially in the areas of adherence to health requests (Chapter 2) and lifestyles (Chapter 7).

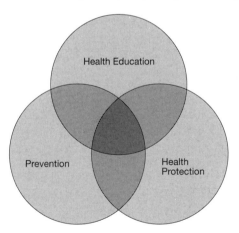

• **Figure 6.2:** Three overlapping areas of health promotion activities, from Tannahill, A. (1985) What is health promotion? *Health Education Journal*, 44, 167–8

PREVENTION

Primary prevention refers to the attempts to combat risk factors before an illness has the chance to develop. *Secondary prevention* refers to the actions which are taken to identify and treat an illness or injury early on, with the aim of stopping or reversing the problem. *Tertiary prevention* involves actions that contain or slow down the damage of serious injury or disease, and, hopefully, rehabilitate the patient. Secondary and tertiary prevention can also involve attempts to improve the quality of life by, for example, reducing pain and increasing mobility.

barriers to primary prevention

The main effort in primary prevention is to either develop programmes to encourage people to change their health-threatening behaviours, or prevent people from developing health-threatening behaviours in the first place. There are, however, a number of barriers to primary prevention including:

- we have only limited knowledge about *what behaviours are threatening* to our health, for example, it is only in the last forty years that we have discovered the very harmful effects of tobacco smoking
- we have a lack of knowledge about *how we develop health-threatening behaviours,* for example, some behaviours to do with diet or exercise develop over many years from our childhood
- a number of health behaviours are *learnt in the home*, for example, the children of smokers are more likely to smoke than the children of non-smokers
- at the *time* that health threatening behaviours develop, people often have little immediate incentive to practice health enhancing behaviours, for example the effects of smoking are felt in middle to later life rather than when people start smoking
- people are often *unrealistically optimistic* about their health (see Chapter 8).

Primary prevention has been largely ignored until very recently, and there are three main reasons for this: first, the traditional structure of Western medicine, second, the difficulty of getting people to practice effective health behaviours, and third, the difficulty in applying methods of attitude and behavioural change to health.

CONTRIBUTIONS FROM PSYCHOLOGY

fear appeals

Discussion of the effects of **fear appeals** usually start with the study by Janis and Feshbach (1953). For their study they prepared three 15-minute illustrated lectures on the dangers of tooth decay and the need for good oral hygiene. The main difference between the three recorded talks was the amount of fear they were designed to create. The *strong fear appeal* emphasised the painful consequences of tooth decay, diseased gums and other dangers such as cancer and blindness that can result from poor oral hygiene. This appeal also included pictures of diseased mouths. The *moderate fear appeal* described the same dangers, but in a less dramatic way and using less disturbing pictures. The *minimal fear appeal* talked about decayed teeth and cavities but did not refer to the serious consequences mentioned in the other appeals, and used diagrams and X-ray pictures rather than photographs.

The results showed that the strong fear appeal did its job and created most worry in the students who received the talk. Also, the strong fear appeal talk was rated as more interesting than the other two talks and the pictures for this talk received a higher rating than the pictures in the other two talks. On the other hand, the strong fear appeal talk also received high negative ratings, with a third of the students saying the pictures were too unpleasant. Overall, then the strong fear appeal produced a strong reaction. However, did it also lead to the biggest change in behaviour? Janis and Feshbach interviewed the students to discover their oral hygiene habits and gave them a 'conformity score' to show how much they had changed their behaviour to follow the advice of the talk. The results showed that the minimal fear appeal created the greatest increase in conformity (36 per cent) and the strong fear appeal created the least (8 per cent).

Although fear appeals seem to have a mixed effect, they still appear frequently in health education messages. The jury is out on whether we should continue to use them, but it is suggested they can be successful if they are combined with other messages. For example, a campaign to prevent the spread of genital warts (be grateful that I've not included the pictures) used a variety of messages to discover which one produced the greatest change in behaviour. The results showed that the fear appeals were effective when they created a sense of threat, and if they produced a sense of **efficacy** ('I can do something about this') with suggestions for a specific change in behaviour (Witte *et al.*, 1998).

The technique of combining the fear message with a self-efficacy message is a common theme in current research, and it appears that the most effective combination is to have a high fear message with a high self-efficacy message (Witte and Allen, 2000). What commonly appears in health education messages, however, is a high fear message with little or no self-efficacy message. A review of messages designed to encourage breast self-examination (BSE) found that the leaflets had an unbalanced proportion of threat to efficacy information. BSE is a technique that women can use to screen themselves for breast cancer, and the alternative screening technique is to use the hi-tech medical procedure called mammography. Interestingly, in the leaflets analysed in the study, the arguments in favour of screening by mammography were very strong, suggesting that there was an underlying aim to encourage the women to seek out medical procedures rather than take control of their own health (Kline and Mattson, 2000).

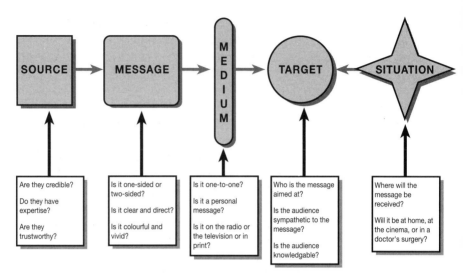

• **Figure 6.3:** The Yale Model of Communication

the yale model of communication

Starting in the 1950s in America a number of psychologists including Carl Hovland investigated the features of a communication that make it persuasive. The work is often summarised as the **Yale Model of Communication**, named after the university where much of the research was carried out. Figure 6.3 shows a brief outline of the model which identifies the important features to consider when preparing a message. These features are: the source of the message (or the persuader), the message, the medium that the message is presented in, the target audience, and the situation in which they will receive the message.

The model attracted a considerable amount of research, though much of it was based on political messages rather than health messages. The general findings from the Yale approach to communication and attitude change were summarised by Zimbardo et al. (1977) who identified the following key suggestions for producing persuasive messages:

1. The source should be *credible*, and the important features of credibility are expertise and trustworthiness. This means that we are more likely to respond to a message from a doctor than we are to a message from a local 'drunk'. It is important to note that someone who is a credible source for a middle-aged professional worker might have no credibility for a young production worker.

2. When an audience is generally positive towards the communicator and the message it is best to present a *one-sided argument*. On the other hand, if the audience is not sympathetic to the message or the communicator then a *two-sided argument* is more effective.

3. There will probably be more changes of opinion in the direction you want if you explicitly *state your conclusions* rather than letting the audience draw their own. The exception to this rule is with a very informed audience, when it is more effective to leave them to draw their own conclusions.
4. The message should be *short*, *clear* and *direct*.
5. The communication should be *colourful* and *vivid* rather than full of technical terms and statistics.
6. The effects of a persuasive communication tend to wear off over time, though attitude change tends to last longer if the person has *actively participated* in the communication rather than just passively receiving it.

The work on fear appeals and message design is still relevant today. It is clear that we will respond to some messages and not to others. You might find it informative to look at some health education material and judge whether it has used any of the psychological findings described above.

other psychological concepts

There are a number of psychological concepts that are important in the understanding of health behaviour and the developing of health promoting campaigns. For example, one of the explanations for the failure of fear appeals is that they create a sense of *learned helplessness* where people feel unable to do anything about their situation. Another issue is *self-efficacy* – if people feel that they are able to carry out successful actions then they are more likely to respond to health messages. An example of this was the 'Back to Sleep' campaign on sudden infant death syndrome (also known as cot death) in which parents were encouraged to put their babies to sleep on their backs rather than on their fronts. This campaign provided a simple action for parents to carry out, and the campaign coincided with, or resulted in, a dramatic fall in the number of sudden infant deaths in the United Kingdom.

Other concepts that help our understanding of health promotion include models of decision-making, locus of control, defence mechanisms, and the model of behavioural change proposed by Prochaska, DiClemente and Norcross (1992).

Section summary

Health promotion involves a wide range of social, medical, psychological and political activities. Psychology has made a contribution to our understanding of some of the processes around health promotion, but its research findings are not always applied to health messages.

Health promotion in schools, worksites and communities

In this section we will look at how psychology has been applied to promoting good health in schools, worksites and communities. Some other examples can also be found elsewhere in the this text, for example the reduction of smoking (Chapter 5), improving adherence to medical advice (Chapter 2), and improving safety at work (Chapter 8).

SCHOOLS

the healthy schools programme

The **Healthy Schools Programme** is part of the current Labour government's drive to improve standards of health and education and to tackle health inequalities. Its aim is to make children, teachers, parents and communities more aware of the opportunities that exist in schools for improving health. The programme was put forward in the document 'Excellence in Schools' (DfEE, 1997) and is part of the 'Our Healthier Nation' policy (DoH, 1999). The most visible feature of this initiative is the Wired for Health website (www.wiredforhealth.gov.uk) which has sites for children at Key Stages 1 to 4, as well as information for teachers and parents. Other components of the healthy schools programme include strategies for safer travel to school and 'cooking for kids'.

One of the starting points for any programme must be to take baseline measures. What are the current health behaviours of children? The answer to this question might well be different in different areas of the country, so local health authorities sometimes collect some very local data. The Health Related Behaviour Questionnaire designed by the Schools Health Education Unit (Balding, 2001) has been used extensively around the UK to measure the health behaviour of young people.

Over 1600 children in North Nottinghamshire completed the form in the summer term of 2000 (NNHA, 2001). The survey found that in the 14–15-year-olds, 12 per cent of boys and 26 per cent of girls saw themselves as regular smokers, though 80 per cent of these smokers wanted to give up. Also in the 14–15-year-olds, 20 per cent said they had an alcoholic drink on three or more days each week, and only 6 per cent did not drink alcohol at all. On economic and environmental issues, 10 per cent of 12–15-year-olds lived in a family without a car, and 27 per cent rated the safety of their area after dark as 'poor' or 'very poor'. The questionnaire also covered relationship and wellbeing issues, and 64 per cent of girls and 16 per cent of boys aged 14–15 said they worry 'a lot' or 'quite a lot' about a range of these issues. The top five worries are shown in Table 6.1

• **Table 6.1:** The top five worries for 14–15-year-olds in North Nottinghamshire (NNHA, 2001)

Problem	Boys (per cent)	Girls (per cent)
career problems	36	46
'the way you look'	21	52
school problems	27	44
family	23	38
health	20	33

Information like this can direct health workers to the areas that require most attention and can suggest public policies that will improve the health of schoolchildren.

peer-based programmes

We prefer to take advice from people like ourselves or from people who we respect. It seems reasonable to suggest, then, that health education programmes led by your peers will be more successful than programmes led by adult strangers or by teachers. Bachman et al. (1988) looked at a health promotion programme where students were asked to talk about drugs to each other, to state their disapproval of drugs and to say that they didn't take drugs. The idea was to create a social norm that was against drug taking and also give people practice in saying 'no'. It was claimed that the programme changed attitudes towards drugs and led to a reduction in cannabis use. A similar programme was reported by Sussman et al. (1995) who compared the effectiveness of teacher-led lessons with lessons that required student participation. The study looked at around 1000 students from schools in the US. Results suggested that there were significant changes in attitudes to drugs and intentions to use drugs in the active participation lessons, but not in the teacher-led lessons.

Two of the criticisms of the peer-led health education programmes are that they are not based on sound theory and do not have much evidence of their effectiveness. There are, however, a number of studies that have compared the effectiveness of peer-led health education in schools with adult-led programmes delivering the same material (Mellanby et al., 2000). It appears that peer-led programmes were at least as effective as the adult-led programmes and sometimes more effective. One of the reasons for this might be that information, particularly of a sensitive kind, is more easily shared between people of a similar age.

WORKSITES

health hazard appraisal

An example of a work-based health programme was introduced at a glass product company in Santa Rosa, California (Rodnick, 1982, cited in Feuerstein, 1986, p. 271). A '**health hazard appraisal**' counselling session was carried out with nearly 300 employees at the company. As part of the programme, full-time staff were offered a comprehensive health examination which included:

- health history
- weight and height measurement
- blood pressure measurement
- range of blood tests including: cholesterol, liver enzyme level, calcium, protein etc.
- TB skin test
- stool test
- physical examination.

This information was used to provide feedback on the risks of contracting various diseases including specific cancers and cardiovascular disease. About two weeks after the tests, the workers attended a group session where they received feedback about their **health-risk profiles**. They were also given information about hypertension, heart disease and cancer.

One year later the workers were tested again and the following improvements in their general health were observed:

- decrease in blood pressure (particularly in individuals with mild hypertension)
- reduction in cholesterol levels in men
- decrease in cigarette smoking
- increase in exercise
- increase in breast self-examination (BSE)
- decrease in alcohol consumption in men
- increase in seat-belt use by men.

smoking reduction

An attempt to encourage people to quit smoking was carried out at five worksites. All the sites received a six-week programme in cognitive behaviour therapy which focused on the skills of giving up. The workers who enrolled in the programmes in four of the sites were put into competing teams, with the workers at the fifth site acting as a control. At the end of the programme 31 per cent of the people in the programme at the control site and 22 per cent at the competition sites had stopped smoking. A follow-up study after six months found that 18 per cent of the control group and 14 per cent of the competition groups had stayed off the cigarettes. This appears to suggest that the control group were doing better than the competition groups, but this was not the case. At the competition sites 88 per cent of the smokers joined the programme, but only 54 per cent did so at the control site, suggesting that the incentive of competition encouraged more people to attempt to give up. When the data was compared for the total number of smokers at each site to give up, there was an overall reduction of 16 per cent at the competition sites and only 7 per cent at the control site (Klesger et al., 1986).

A worksite intervention that has grown in popularity is to ban smoking at work. One of the questions to consider about this policy is whether smokers reduce their consumption because of the ban, or whether they simply adjust their behaviour and smoke at different times. A smoking ban in Australian ambulance crews was monitored by **self-report measures**, and also by physiological measures such as blood and exhaled carbon dioxide. The measures were taken just before the ban, just after it, and again six weeks later. The self-report results showed that the ambulance crews reported less smoking both at the start of the ban and after six weeks. The physiological measures, however, returned to the baseline measures after six weeks, suggesting that the smokers were finding other times to smoke, or were maybe finding secret places to smoke while at work (Gomel et al., 1993). This suggests that worksite smoking bans might well be useful in changing behaviour at work, and also improving the quality of life for non-smokers, but their overall effectiveness in reducing smoking is far less clear.

The problem of measuring the effectiveness of worksite health promotion is a general one that goes beyond 'quit smoking' programmes. A review of over 100 programmes of worksite health promotion found that only a quarter of them were initiated in response to the needs or views of the workers, and very few involved partnerships between workers and employers. Most of the programmes were aimed at changing individual behaviour and did not include any changes in the working environment or working practices to encourage these behaviours. The review also noticed a gap between what was regarded as 'good practice' and what has been found to be effective in research studies (Harden, et al., 1999). I guess this means that, as with many other health interventions, people do what they believe to be the *right thing*, rather than what research has told us is the *best thing*.

COMMUNITIES

coronary heart disease and mass media appeals

It is difficult to evaluate the effect of **mass media appeals**. In the case of product advertising the effect can be measured in sales. In the case of health behaviour it is difficult to come up with appropriate measures since there are so many influences on us every day. One of the most famous studies on the effectiveness of mass media messages was the Stanford Heart Disease Prevention Programme (see, for example Farquhar et al., 1977). This study looked at three similar small towns in the US. Two of the towns received a massive media campaign concerning smoking, diet and exercise over a two-year period. This campaign used television, radio, newspapers, posters and mailshots. The third town had no campaign and so acted as a control.

The researchers interviewed several hundred people in the three towns between the ages of 35 and 60. They were interviewed before the campaign began, after one year, and again after two years when the campaign ended. The interviews included questions about health behaviours, knowledge about the risks of heart disease, and physical measures such as blood pressure and cholesterol levels. In one of the two campaign towns, the researchers used the interview data to identify over one hundred people who were at high risk of heart disease and offered them one-to-one counselling.

The people in the control town showed a slight increase in risk factors for heart disease, and the people in the campaign towns showed a moderate decrease. The campaign produced increased awareness of the dangers of heart disease but produced relatively little change in behaviour. The exception to this was the people who had been offered one-to-one counselling – this group showed significant changes in behaviour. This study suggests that mass media campaigns by themselves produce only small changes in behaviour, but they can act as a cue to positive action if further encouragement is offered.

reducing skin cancer risk

Over the past twenty years there has been a large growth in the incidence of skin cancers, which might be due to a combination of changes in the environment and changes in lifestyles. There are a number of health promotion campaigns to encourage safe behaviours in the sun. A study on the effectiveness of these programmes was carried out by McClendon and Prentice (2001). White students who chose to tan were given a health promotion intervention based on protection motivation theory (PMT). The intervention was made up of brief lectures, an essay, short discussions and a video about a young man who died of melanoma (a particularly dangerous form of skin cancer). There were two sessions, each just over one hour long and taking place two days apart.

The researchers used psychometric tests to estimate responses to a range of variables including:

- vulnerability
- severity of the threat
- self-efficacy
- costs and rewards
- intentions.

With the exception of self-efficacy, these variables all showed some significant change after the intervention and remained effective one month later. However, the issue is not whether people intend to change their behaviour, but whether they actually do change their behaviour. This is always more difficult to measure. In this study, however, they took photographs of the participants at the start of the study and again after one month. These pairs of photographs were then judged by four blind-raters (judges who did not know whether the pictures were before or after) to see whether the students' skin had tanned further or become lighter. The students were not aware that this judgement would take place. Of the 32 individuals photographed, 23 (72 per cent) were judged to have lighter skin tone after one month, 4 (12.5 per cent) were rated as having no change and 5 (16 per cent) were judged to have darker skin.

homelessness

Not everybody has equal access to healthcare. Some members of our society are socially excluded from the wealth and health that most people enjoy. One group of people who fall into this category is the homeless, and one of the challenges for health promotion is to create initiatives that deal with their needs. The health status of homeless people is very poor compared to the general population (Plearce and Quilgares, 1996). This is true for diet, malnutrition, substance misuse, mental health problems, infectious diseases (such as tuberculosis), cardiovascular disease, accidents and hypothermia. Homeless people commonly come to the attention of health workers only when they develop an illness rather than through screening procedures, and they often use accident and emergency departments to deal with their health problems (Power et al., 1999). As a result they are often missed by the regular health promotion programmes.

There are a number of barriers to health promotion for homeless people including (Power et al., 1999):

- workers with homeless people are often isolated and there is not very much collaboration between the various agencies that work with the homeless
- health promotion units do not set up many initiatives aimed specifically at homelessness and housing
- homeless people can feel alienated from health education messages as they often require a high level of literacy
- although homeless people are concerned about health problems, issues such as low self-esteem and low expectations can prevent them from taking part in heath promoting activities.

The issue of homelessness highlights the breadth of health promotion. If we are to deal with the health needs of people who are excluded from society then we have to deal with the reasons for exclusion as well as with illness prevention and treatment. To state the obvious – this is easier said than done.

Section summary   There have been numerous health promotion programmes in schools, worksites and communities with various levels of success. It remains difficult to assess the effectiveness of such programmes but there is a general belief that they are good thing.

Issues in health promotion

In this section, we will look at two issues in health promotion that raise some dilemmas about health promotion and how it will develop in the future.

CYBERDOCS

At the end of the 20th century there was an exponential growth of medical web pages and databases (Eysenbach *et al.*, 2001) and this growth shows no sign of abating. It appears that medical sites provide some of the most visited areas of the internet. Survey data from 1998 (reported in Eysenbach *et al.*, 2001) shows that 27 per cent of women and 15 per cent of men said they accessed medical information on the internet weekly or daily. There are currently in excess of 100,000 medical websites, and when I typed in 'cancer' to the Google search engine in the spring of 2001 I got over 6.7 million results. What this means is that the way we get information about health is changing quite substantially. For example, there is a growth in the number of patient–patient interactions as people share their symptoms and e; with others who have the same or a similar condition. There is also growing tendency for people to download health information before the doctor's surgery, thereby changing the relationship between do patient (Bader and Braude, 1998; Kahn, 1997).

One potential benefit of on-line healthcare comes from the uniqu people access information on the internet (Grohol, 1998). People communicate and behave differently when using computers compare equivalent behaviours in other situations, such as face to face interac...... The Samaritans report that while around 20 per cent of telephone callers report suicidal thoughts, this figure increases to around 50 per cent of e-mail contacts (*The Scotsman*, 24th February, 1999). GPs and patients have been shown to behave differently during medical consultations when a desktop computer is used in the diagnostic process (Als, 1997; Greatbatch *et al.*, 1995). People communicating using computers have been found to be more hostile, less inhibited, and more likely to self-disclose than people communicating face to face (for a review see Joinson, 1998). People are also more willing to swap personal information (Parks and Floyd, 1996) and to publish details about themselves that are normally protected (Joinson, 1998).

One of the key issues with internet-based information is quality control. When we go to the doctor's surgery we have a high degree of confidence in the staff working there. When we access the internet we commonly have no idea who are dealing with unless we access a branded site – such as CancerHelp (www.cancerhelp.org.uk). Some research has looked at the quality of websites (Impicciatore et al., 1997), newsgroups (Culver et al., 1997, cited in Eysenbach et al, 2001), and evaluated sites that offer personal consultations (Eysenbach and Diepgen 1998). All these studies have found that the reliability, completeness and accessibility of the information and advice is very variable and can range from the helpful to the dangerous. It might well be that in the future some sort of quality kitemark can be introduced so that people can tell whether a site is giving sound advice backed up by research, biased advice from commercial concerns, or plain stupid advice from rank amateurs. However you look at it though, the face of health promotion is changing radically as the general public get more and more access to medical information.

SCREENING

Screening is the attempt to detect an illness early so that treatment can prevent it developing and maybe give a better chance of cure. It became increasingly important throughout the 20th century, although recently there has been growing resistance to it. It is generally thought to be a good thing (Ogden, 2000) as long as:

- the disease is common enough and serious enough to make it worthwhile
- accurate diagnosis is possible
- early diagnosis is helpful
- there is a test that is sensitive enough and specific enough
- it is an illness that can remain undetected or undiagnosed for a while.

Psychologists have been particularly interested in the decision to screen as it is clear that some groups of people are less likely to screen than others. A study on the screening choices of nearly 400 women from Northern Ireland (Murray and McMillan, 1993) looked at a range of measures including: their screening behaviour, their health beliefs, their health locus of control, and their emotional control. They found that women were more likely to self-examine their breasts if they were young, from the professional classes, did not have a great belief in the role of powerful others (such as doctors), believed in the benefits of treatment, and had good knowledge about cervical and breast cancer. They were also more likely to breast self-examine if they attended cervical smear clinics. Attendance at cervical smear clinics was affected by a similar a range of variables with the addition of religious beliefs having a positive effect on attendance.

problems with screening

Some screening procedures bring with them a small risk of personal harm. For example, it has been suggested that the procedure of mammography has a low level of risk and that if 40 million women were screened every year for 20 years, then 120 would die from radiation-induced breast cancer (Strax 1978), though Ogden (2000) points out that since these concerns were raised the level of radiation used has been reduced.

There are also some psychological costs involved in taking part in screening procedures (Marteau, 1993; Wardle and Pope, 1992) including:

- the effects of taking part in medical procedures, such as worry about the procedure, anxiety about possible distressing results, and fear that the invitation to attend implies an illness in the patient
- effects of getting negative (no illness) results, including raising concerns about mortality, and creating high levels of reassurance
- effects of positive (illness) results, including anxiety, fear and depression
- effects of false positive results, including anxieties about the disease and anger at the distress caused by screening (see below).

ultrasound screening: reactions to false positive results

Screening is fine so long as you get a good result. Baillie *et al.* (2000) interviewed women who received a **false positive result** of an ultrasound test (a false positive occurs when you are told there might be something wrong but it turns out to be alright in the end). Many people look forward to ultrasound screening during pregnancy because they see it as a chance to confirm their pregnancy and get the first pictures for the family album. In fact one of the participants said they were looking forward to it because 'everyone kept saying it's the best part of your pregnancy'. Although parents see the scan as almost a fun thing, it has a medical objective, and that is to check the health of the baby and look for chromosomal abnormalities. The screening techniques are good at spotting abnormalities such as Down's Syndrome, but fewer than 2 per cent of the screens identified as 'high risk' turn out to have an abnormality. This means that a large number of women are told their baby has a high risk of abnormality, but subsequently this turns out to be not the case. The women who received a false positive result described what an unsettling experience it was for them. Many remained anxious throughout the pregnancy, even after further tests had contradicted the original scan.

False positives can have an effect on the general well-being of the mother and they can also have serious medical consequences. As a result of the false positive result, other tests might be performed, such as amniocentesis, which has a small but significant risk of damage to the foetus.

Section summary

The promotion of good health seems to be a fairly straightforward ambition, but scratch the surface and you come up with a number of puzzling ideas. One of these is the idea that 'prevention is better than cure'. Well yes, that might seem to be the case, but what if the prevention is a programme of mass immunisation of all children to reduce a damaging but rarely fatal disease, and what if that immunisation programme prevents a handful of deaths but at the same time opens up the risk of a reaction to the injection? You prevent illness in some people by opening other people to a new risk of illness.

KEY TERMS

efficacy
false positive result
fear appeals
health hazard appraisal
health-risk profile
Healthy Schools Programme
mass media appeals
primary prevention
screening
self-report measures
Yale Model of Communication

EXERCISE 1

Pick up some leaflets from your local surgery and see whether they follow the psychological principles outlined in this chapter. For example, do they make fear appeals and do they use credible sources?

EXERCISE 2

Design two leaflets to encourage people to eat fruit. One should be aimed at school children and the other at clubbers. What are the differences between the two leaflets?

(a) Describe what psychologists have found out health promotion.

(b) Discuss the psychological evidence on health promotion.

(c) Suggest one psychological technique for promoting the eating of fresh fruit. Give reasons for your answer.

Further reading

If you want a weighty and thorough text then pick up Donaldson, L.J. and Donaldson, R.J. (2000) *Essential public health*, 2nd ed. Newbury: Petroc Press.

A more concise summary of some of the key issues can be found in Bennett, P. and Murphy, S. (1997) *Psychology and health promotion*. Buckingham: Open University Press.

Websites

Health promotion takes many forms on the internet. It might be worth visiting some of the large charitable foundations that produce information on specific health problems, for example the British Heart Foundation and Cancer Help:
www.bhf.org.uk
www.cancerhelp.org.uk

Self-efficacy is a concept that appears throughout this text. You can find out more about this idea at:
www.emory.edu/EDUCATION/mfp/effpage.html

Lifestyles and health behaviour

Introduction

Why do we behave in the way we do? What things encourage us to look after our health, and what things encourage us to be careless with it? When we attempt to find some answers it is helpful to make a distinction between the situation factors (such as where we live, and what communities we belong to) and personal factors (such as our attitudes to health and the value we put on health).

THIS CHAPTER EXAMINES:

- determinants of health behaviours
  - poverty
  - type A behaviour
  - religiosity
- health belief models
- developmental, cultural and gender differences.

Determinants of health behaviours

HEALTH AND POVERTY

It is important to point out that the most damaging **lifestyles** for our health are those associated with low incomes. Throughout the Western world, the most consistent predictor of illness and early death is income. People who are unemployed, homeless, or on low incomes have higher rates of all the major causes of premature death (Fitzpatrick and Dollamore, 1999; Carroll, Davey Smith and Bennett, 1994). The reasons for this are not clear although there are two main lines of argument. First, it is possible that people with low incomes engage in risky behaviours more frequently, so they might smoke more cigarettes and drink more alcohol. This argument probably owes more to negative stereotypes of working-class people than it does to any systematic research.

The second line of argument is that poor people are exposed to greater health risks in the environment in the form of hazardous jobs and poor living accommodation. Also, people on low incomes will probably buy cheaper foods which have a higher content of fat (regarded as a risk factor for coronary heart disease). All this means that psychological interventions on behaviour can only have a limited effect, since it is economic circumstances that most affect the health of the nation.

The effects of **poverty** are long-lasting and far-reaching. A remarkable study by Dorling et al. (2000) compared late 20th century death rates in London with modern patterns of poverty, and also with patterns of poverty from the late 19th century. The researchers used information from Charles Booth's survey of inner London carried out in 1896, and matched it to modern local government records. When they looked at the recent **mortality** (death) rates from diseases that are commonly associated with poverty (such as stomach cancer, stroke and lung cancer), they found that the measures of deprivation from 1896 were even more strongly related to them than the deprivation measures from the 1990s. They concluded that patterns of disease must have their roots in the past. It is remarkable, but true, that geographical patterns of social deprivation and disease are so strong that a century of change in inner London has not disrupted them.

Another study by Dorling et al. (2001) plotted the mortality ratio (rate of deaths compared to the national average) against voting patterns in the 1997 general election. They divided the constituencies into ten categories, ranging from those who had the highest Labour vote to those who had the lowest. The analysis found that the constituencies with the highest Labour vote (72 per cent on average) had the highest mortality ratio (127), and that this ratio decreased in line with the proportion of people voting Labour, down to the lower Labour vote (22 per cent on average) where there was a much lower mortality ratio (84). This means that early death, and presumably poor health, was more common in areas that chose to vote Labour. If we take Labour voting as still being influenced by class and social status then this study gives us another measure of the effects of wealth on health.

The influence of poverty shows up in a number of ways. Glaucoma is a damaging eye disease that can cause blindness if untreated. A study by Fraser et al. (2001) looked at the differences between people who sought medical help early (early presenters) and those who sought help for the first time when the disease was already quite advanced (late presenters). The late presenters were more likely to be in lower occupational classes, more likely to have left full-time education at age 14 or younger, more likely to be tenants than owner occupiers, and less likely to have access to a car. It showed that a person's personal circumstances and the area they lived in had an effect on their decision to seek help with their vision. It also appeared that the disease developed more quickly in people with low incomes.

One uncomfortable explanation of the differences in mortality rates for rich and poor might be that the poor receive worse treatment from the NHS. Affluent women have a higher incidence of breast cancer than women who are socially deprived, but they have a better chance of survival. A study to investigate the care of the breast cancer patients from the most and least well-off areas in Glasgow was carried out by Macleod *et al.* (2000). They looked at records from hospital and general practice to evaluate the treatment that was given, the delay between consultation and treatment, and the type and frequency of follow-up care. The data showed that women from the affluent areas did not receive better care from the NHS. The women from the deprived areas received similar treatment, were admitted to hospital more often for other conditions than the cancer, and had more consultations after the treatment than the women from the affluent areas. Perhaps the reasons for the worse survival rate of women from deprived areas are not related to the quality of care, but to the number and severity of *other* diseases that they have alongside the cancer.

THE TYPE A BEHAVIOUR PATTERN

Do some lifestyles make people more vulnerable to disease? Are we justified, for example, in associating high stress behaviour with certain health problems such as heart disease? Friedman and Rosenman (1959) investigated this and created a description of behaviour patterns that has generated a large amount of research and also become part of the general discussions on health in popular magazines.

Before we look at the work of Friedman and Rosenman, it is worth making a psychological distinction between behaviour patterns and personality. Textbooks and articles often refer to the Type A *personality*, though, at least in the original paper, the authors describe it as a *behaviour pattern* rather than a *personality type*. The difference between these two is that a personality type is what *you are*, whereas a behaviour pattern is what *you do*. The importance of this distinction comes in our analysis of why we behave in a particular way ('I was made this way' or 'I learnt to be this way'), and what can be done about it. It is easier to change a person's pattern of learnt behaviour than it is to change their nature.

Friedman and Rosenman devised a description of **Pattern A behaviour** that they expected to be associated with high levels of blood cholesterol and hence coronary heart disease. This description was based on their previous research and their clinical experience with patients. A summary of Pattern A behaviour is given below:

(1)   an intense, sustained drive to *achieve* personal (and often poorly defined) goals
(2)   a profound tendency and eagerness to *compete* in all situations
(3)   a persistent desire for *recognition* and advancement
(4)   continuous involvement in several activities at the same time that are constantly subject to *deadlines*
(5)   an habitual tendency to *rush* to finish activities
(6)   extraordinary mental and physical *alertness*.

Pattern B behaviour, on the other hand, is the opposite of Pattern A, characterised by the relative absence of drive, ambition, urgency, desire to compete, or involvement in deadlines.

research into type A behaviour

The classic study of Type A and Type B behaviour patterns was a twelve-year longitudinal study of over 3,500 healthy middle-aged men reported by Friedman and Rosenman in 1974. They found that, compared to people with the Type B behaviour pattern, people with the Type A behaviour pattern were twice as likely to develop coronary heart disease. Other researchers found that differences in the kinds of Type A behaviour correlated with different kinds of heart disease: angina sufferers tended to be impatient and intolerant with others, while those with heart failure tended to be hurried and rushed, inflicting the pressures on themselves.

A study by Ragland and Brand (1988) illustrates how complex the relationship is between behaviour and coronary heart disease. In their original study they found that measures of Type A behaviour were useful in predicting the development of coronary heart disease. However, in the follow-up study conducted 22 years later, the initial behaviour pattern of the men was compared with their subsequent mortality rates. Ragland and Brand found that among the 231 men who survived the first coronary event for 24 hours or more, those who had initially displayed a Type A behaviour pattern died at a much lower rate than the men who displayed a Type B behaviour pattern (19.1 versus 31.7 per 1000 person-years). This finding was rather unexpected and seems to contradict the general view about Type A behaviour. One explanation is that people who display the Type A behaviour pattern may respond differently to a heart attack than people who display the Type B behaviour pattern. Alternatively, Type A behaviour patterns may cease to be a risk factor after such an event. People may take the warning and change their lifestyle.

Recent reviews of Type A behaviour suggest that it is not a useful measure for predicting whether someone will have a heart attack or not. Myrtek (2001), for example, looked at a wide range of studies on this issue and concluded that measures of Type A and of hostility were so weakly associated with

Classifying behaviour into Type A or Type B is usually done by interview or by questionnaire. Examples of questions are:

1 **'Has your partner or friend ever told you that you eat too fast?'**
   Type A's are likely to say, 'Yes, often'.
   Type B's are likely to say, 'Yes, once or twice' or 'No'.

2 **'How would your partner, or best friend, rate your general level of activity?'**
   Type A's are likely to say, 'Too active, need to slow down'.
   Type B's are likely to say, 'Too slow, need to be more active'.

3 **'Do you ever set deadlines or quotas for yourself at work or at home?'**
   Type A's are likely to say, 'Yes, once a week or more often'.
   Type B's are likely to say, 'Only occasionally'.

4 **'When you are in the middle of a job and someone (not your boss) interrupts you, how do you feel inside?'**
   Type A's are likely to say, 'I feel irritated because most interruptions are unnecessary'.
   Type B's are likely to say, 'I feel O.K. because I work better after an occasional break'.

• **Figure 7.1:** Type A and Type B behaviour patterns

coronary heart disease as to make them no use for prevention or prediction. The lasting appeal of the Type A behaviour pattern is its simplicity and plausibility (an example of the types of question used to judge the behaviour pattern are given in Figure 7.1). Unfortunately, health is rarely that simple and the interaction of stress with physiological, psychological, social and cultural factors cannot be reduced to two simple behaviour patterns.

RELIGIOSITY AND HEALTH

Religious beliefs have been connected with health for a long time. In fact, the word 'health' comes from the same root as the word 'holy'. In the modern world, where we tend to look for medical answers to our problems rather than spiritual ones, it is unusual to consider the healthy effects of being religious. You might think that this would be a matter of belief rather than science, but you would be wrong. It is possible to look at the health of people with different lifestyle choices, and one of these choices is their religion.

In 1921 Lewis Terman started the Terman Life-Cycle Study looking at the lives of over 1500 people. The sample was recruited from schools in California after the teachers identified children who were gifted and had an IQ of 135 and above. The average year of birth was 1910 so their age at the start of the study was 11 years. It was not a very diverse sample, as they were mostly selected from white middle-class families, but this apparent weakness is a strength if we want to look at the effect of selected variables that do not include ethnicity and class. Data was collected over the years and in 1950 (when the participants were aged about 40) they were asked about their **religiosity** on a four-point scale (not at all: little: moderate: strong). Forty years later the researchers were able to compare this data against the mortality of the sample. To cut to the chase, once the researchers had accounted for all the other variables they were able to say that people who were more religious lived longer (Clark *et al.*, 1999).

Section summary   A number of factors contribute to our health behaviour. These include the situation we are in (for example, poverty), our patterns of behaviour (for example, the Type A), and our beliefs (for example, religiosity).

Health belief models

There are a number of models of health behaviour including: the health belief model, the theory of reasoned action, the theory of planned behaviour, protection motivation theory, and subjective expected utility theory. All the theories have some value although none of them provides a comprehensive model of health behaviour. For a review see Weinstein (1993), or Armitage and Conner (2000). In this section we will concentrate on the health belief model as an example of these behavioural theories.

THE HEALTH BELIEF MODEL

The **Health Belief Model** (Becker and Rosenstock, 1984) suggests that the likelihood that a person will carry out a behaviour that will protect their health depends on two assessments (see Figure 7.2):

EVALUATING THE THREAT

When we are confronted with a health risk we evaluate our personal threat by considering how serious the condition is (*perceived seriousness*), and how likely we are to get it (*perceived vulnerability*). For example, if a person is overweight they might be in danger of developing a heart condition. The person would probably recognise this as a serious condition, but they might believe that because they are still quite young they are unlikely to develop this problem just yet. Therefore they might judge the threat as relatively low.

Even if we judge the threat to be serious, we are only likely to act if we have some cue to action. This cue might be a physical symptom like developing chest pains, or it might be a mass media campaign, or it might be the death of a colleague with heart disease.

COST–BENEFITS ANALYSIS

The other assessment is a cost–benefit analysis which looks at whether the *perceived benefits* of changing our behaviour exceed the perceived barriers. The barriers might be financial, situational (difficult to get to a health clinic), or social (don't want to acknowledge getting old). The benefits might be improved health, relief from anxiety, and reduction of health risks.

applying the health belief model

One of the big health campaigns of the 1980s aimed to encourage people, especially young people, to use condoms in their sexual behaviour to reduce the threat of HIV and AIDS. In a study of over 300 sexually active Scottish teenagers, Abraham *et al.* (1992) looked at how the various components of the health belief model related to the intentions and behaviour of the young people. They found that the perceived seriousness of HIV infection, the perceived vulnerability, and the perceived effectiveness of condoms had little effect on their behaviour. The factors that had the greatest effect on their intentions and behaviour were the costs of condom use. These costs included beliefs about pleasure reduction, awkwardness of use and the likely response from their partner if they suggested using a condom. These findings suggest that the early campaigns that emphasised vulnerability and threat had little effect on the behaviour of sexually active people, and that it would be more effective to concentrate campaigns on the barriers to condom use.

The health belief model has attracted a large amount of research and much of it is supportive of the basic theory. However, there is no standard way of measuring the variables in the model such as **perceived susceptibility**.

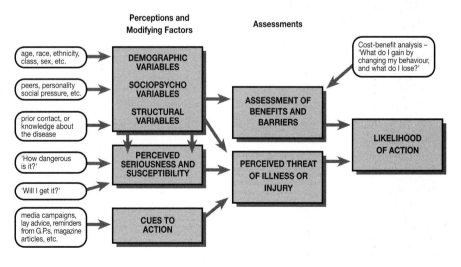

• **Figure 7.2:** The Health Belief Model

Also, there are a number of health behaviours that do not fit the model, such as habits like teeth brushing. This means that the model has limited value in predicting whether people will comply with health requests, but it has been useful in trying to understand why people choose the health behaviours that they do.

A more serious criticism comes from Smedslund (2000) who argues that the various health belief models are not quite what they are made out to be. He argues that many of the assumptions in the theories are true by definition, or are based on assumptions that cannot be tested. For example, in the Health Belief Model it is suggested that your prior knowledge of a disease will affect your perception of how susceptible you are to it. When you think about it, however, you realise that if you do not know anything about the disease then you cannot feel susceptible to it. So prior knowledge is not a factor that affects how susceptible you feel, but a factor that must be there for you to feel any susceptibility at all. To summarise, he argues that many of the research studies into the effectiveness of these theories end up supporting hypotheses that need no support. He suggests that the theories have a psycho-logic which means they are bound to be supported by any evidence that is collected. Smedslund argues that studies to test these theories are pointless because the theories are necessarily true. This kind of heresy could put us all out of a job – so I will pass quickly on!

COGNITIVE APPROACHES TO HEALTH

locus of control

How much control do you think you have over your behaviour, your environment or your health? Psychologists believe that the amount of control that we *perceive* ourselves to have is very important to us. Rotter (1966) first described the concept of **locus of control** and applied it to range of activities such as gambling, political activism and hospitalisation. He suggested that people differ in the way they experience their locus of control – in other words, where the control over events in their life comes from. Some people experience themselves as having an *external locus of control*, which means they do not feel in control of events. They perceive their lives as being controlled by outside forces; in other words, things happen to them. On the other hand, some people experience themselves as having an *internal locus of control*, which means they experience themselves as having personal control over themselves and events; in other words, they do things.

health locus of control

The concept of *locus of control* was measured using a series of statements that people could either agree or disagree with. However, it soon became apparent that people's control beliefs about their health were quite different from their control beliefs about other aspects of their behaviour. So, health psychologists such as Wallston *et al.* (1978) expanded the original scale beyond the simple external–internal dimension to develop health-specific psychometric tests. The Multidimensional Health Locus of Control Scale measures three dimensions of health locus of control:

INTERNALITY: the extent to which locus of control for health is internal (example statement: *If I become sick, I have the power to make myself well again*).

CHANCE: the belief that chance or external factors are affecting the outcome of health problems (example statement: *Often I feel sick no matter what I do. If I am going to get sick, I will get sick*).

POWERFUL OTHERS: the belief in the control of powerful others (such as doctors) over our health (example statement: *Following doctor's orders to the letter is the best way for me to stay healthy*).

A study on the relationship between health locus of control (HLC) and health protective behaviours was carried out by survey on over 11,000 people from Wales (Norman *et al.*, 1998). They collected data on the three dimensions of health locus of control, and also on health behaviours with regard to:

- smoking
- alcohol
- exercise
- diet – eating fruit.

They divided the people into eight types on the basis of their HLC scores (calculated by the combination of high or low scores they got on the three variables). The results showed that the 'pure internal' group (high on the internal scale, high on the powerful other scale, and low on the chance scale) and the 'nay-sayers' group (low on all three measures) carried out more health protective behaviours than the other groups.

The health locus of control scales provide a simple way of investigating the effect of beliefs on health outcomes. Consequently there has been a large amount of research using these scales, although the relationship between health locus of control and health outcome has not been as strong as we might have expected. One reason for this is that people have very different perceptions of their control over different areas of their health. For example, I may feel in control of my diet but unable to control my alcohol consumption. To deal with this problem, some scales have been developed that are even more specific, and look at more detailed beliefs such as perceived control over pain.

self-efficacy

Self-efficacy is a belief that you can perform adequately in a particular situation. Your sense of personal competence influences your perception, motivation and performance. Bandura (1977) suggested that self-efficacy beliefs are important to us, because they are concerned with what we believe we are capable of. If we believe that we are able to engage in certain types of actions successfully, then we are more likely to put effort into carrying them out, and therefore we are more likely to develop the necessary skills.

It seems likely that beliefs about our self-efficacy will affect how much effort we put into any activity. In the area of health, if we do not believe that we can change our lifestyle and, for example, give up smoking, then we will probably not even try. Bandura suggested that it is a good thing if people have beliefs about their self-efficacies which are slightly higher than the evidence would suggest (in other words, they think they are a little more capable than they really are). This encourages them to aim high, and, by doing so, to try harder and so develop their skills and abilities even further.

We make judgements of self-efficacy primarily on the basis of our achievements. Other sources of these judgements include:

(a)   Observations of the performance of others ('Well if she can do it, then so can I')
(b)   Social and self persuasion ('Oh, you know you can do it really')
(c)   Monitoring our emotional states. For example, if we are feeling anxious then this would suggest low expectations of efficacy ('I don't feel up to it today').

An example of a study that looks at the role of self-efficacy was an investigation into the use of condoms by college students (Wulfert and Wan, 1993). They found that their sample of students was well-informed about the health risks of unprotected sex, and the facts and myths of AIDS transmission. They found that knowledge had little effect on sexual behaviour and many of the students made inconsistent use of condoms. The factor that was the best predictor of condom use was, in fact, self-efficacy, or in other words, whether the students felt they could use a condom and still have a successful sexual encounter. This suggests that health education on the use of condoms should not concentrate on the health risks of unprotected sex but on encouraging a sense of self-efficacy in potential condom users.

NON-RATIONAL EXPLANATIONS

One of the criticisms of the health belief models and the cognitive explanations is that they assume that people think and behave in relatively logical and rational ways. You don't have to reflect on your own behaviour for too long to find some examples of behaviour that were far from rational. We will consider two examples of **non-rational explanations**, first optimism and second magic.

optimism

One of the problems that health educators have to deal with when they are trying to change an individual's behaviour is our unrealistic **optimism** about our health. A number of studies, for example Weinstein (1987), have asked people to rate their personal risk of developing various disorders compared to people like them. Individuals usually rate their chances of illness as less than that of other people. The problem with this optimism is illustrated in a study by Turner *et al.* (1988) of students at Oxford University who judged their own risk of contracting AIDS to be less than that of their fellow students. This was even true of students who were taking part in high risk behaviours such as unprotected penetrative sex, and sex with bisexual partners, intravenous drug users, or prostitutes. So, why are we so optimistic about our health? Weinstein suggested four cognitive factors that affect this optimism:

(i)   people tend to believe that if a problem has not appeared yet, then it is unlikely to develop in the future
(ii)   people tend to think that personal action can prevent the problem
(iii) people believe that the problem is rare
(iv)   people have little or no experience of the problem.

These cognitive factors do not provide a logical framework for making judgements about personal risk, but people do not operate on the basis of logic. On the whole, this optimism is no bad thing since it prevents us from developing a maudlin preoccupation with illness, but it does mean that we are resistant to health messages about the dangers of our lifestyle.

Theme link: Application of psychology to everyday life

Magical beliefs and food
We might think we are rational people, but we commonly respond to superstitious ideas and folk beliefs. Many instructions about the use of food that appear in the popular press have more to do with magical thinking than science. For example, the idea that impurities and toxins will be stored in the body unless we take action to purify ourselves, or that we should eat a diet that has approximately 70 per cent water because we are made up of 70 per cent water.

The **laws of magic** assume that things act on each other at a distance through a secret sympathy (Lindeman, 2000). There are two laws of sympathetic magic: the law of contagion and the law of similarity. The law of contagion holds that things that have been in contact with each other continue to act on each other at a distance after the contact has been broken. This contagion can be either negative (for example, contamination and pollution, so people with cancer sometimes find that colleagues and friends are reluctant to touch them or use the same coffee cup) or positive (for example a lucky charm, or colour therapy).

Contamination beliefs may sometimes have a real-world basis, but the main difference between magic and science is (a) the power of the contamination is exaggerated, and (b) the contaminant is thought to leave a permanent trace. Imagine finding two plates of food with some toppings you don't want on them (a) sterilised cockroach or (b) some baked beans. You might well eat Plata (b) after removing the beans, but you will probably refuse to eat Plata (a), even though the cockroach is sterilised and will leave no trace.

The second law of magical thinking, the law of similarity, holds that superficial resemblances indicate or cause deeper resemblances. To put it another way, the image equals the object. So we might be suggestible to the idea that heart-shaped leaves can treat heart disease and a drug made from the lung of a fox can treat respiratory problems. Working on this principle, my tip is to avoid all magical treatments for piles.

Section summary   Psychology has developed a number of explanations for our health behaviour. These explanations have been used with limited success to encourage people to improve their health.

Developmental, cultural and gender differences in health behaviours

The research on individual differences in health is vast and covers a very wide range of issues. The following studies illustrate just a few of these, and you will notice that there is some overlap between the categories.

DEVELOPMENTAL DIFFERENCES

fetal alcohol syndrome

Health issues for children start before they are born. It is important for the developing child to have a good level of nutrition and be relatively free from drugs and alcohol. An example of the consequences of early disadvantage is **fetal alcohol syndrome** (FAS). The symptoms of FAS are head and facial abnormalities, brain damage, low birthweight, hearing problems and impairment of growth. The syndrome is commonly associated with the children of alcoholic mothers, and there may well be other issues as well as alcohol that create the problems. For example, the alcoholic mother might not be eating well, sleeping well, or attending antenatal clinics. Research studies with animals, however, can use controlled experiments to estimate the effect on alcohol on the young. Studies on rats have found that one binge-drinking episode early in pregnancy is enough to create a measurable effect in 50 per cent of births (Sulik *et al.*, 1981), and also measurable differences in brain structure in the regions associated with long-term memory (Dumas, 1994).

There is growing awareness in the UK and the US about the effects of alcohol in pregnancy, and a number of programmes have been targeted at women drinkers, though with mixed success (Murphy *et al.*, 1999). The health promotion work deals with two issues, reducing alcohol use in pregnant women (Abel *et al.*, 1998), and helping children born with FAS. Psychologists have developed a psychometric measure to estimate the effects of FAS (Streissguth *et al.*, 1998), and use it to predict the ability of children with FAS to live independently when they reach adulthood. There is also an increasing amount of material on how to overcome the effects of FAS (for example, Kanter and Streissguth, 1997).

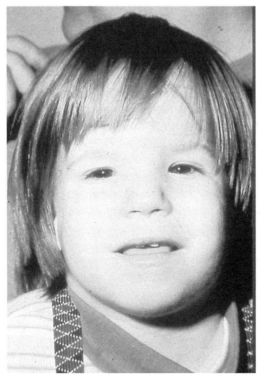

Figure 7.3: Picture of a child with fetal alcohol syndrome. Streissguth, Landesman-Dwyer, Martin and Smith (1980). Teratogenic effects of alcohol in humans and laboratory animals. *Science*, 209, 18, 353–361

child survival

An application of psychology outside the Western world has been in the UNICEF strategy to improve the rates of child survival. The strategy is called GOBI after the first words of the four points listed below (Harkness *et al.*, 1988);

1. Growth monitoring to identify early cases of malnutrition and failure to grow.
2. Oral rehydration therapy for infants and children with severe diarrhoea. Diarrhoea is a major cause of death in poor countries, and was in fact the major cause of infant death in British cities until the turn of the 20th century. The therapy reduces the high rate of death from fluid loss.
3. Breast-feeding promotion, because breast milk is high in nutrition, and also helps to immunise the baby from some common diseases. Breast-feeding also reduces the chances of infection from unsterilised bottles.
4. Immunisation against the major childhood infectious diseases.

Psychology can make a major contribution to this programme, especially in the promotion of breast-feeding. This behaviour is full of social meanings and it is not enough to present a direct message in the terminology of Western medicine. Fernandez and Guthrie (1983, cited in Berry *et al.*, 1992) suggest that it is important to take account of **lay beliefs** about health when education programmes are designed. If the programme describes traditional behaviours and beliefs as harmful, then it is unlikely that local people will respond to the message. There is also the counter pressure from multinational companies who encourage women to buy their baby milk, despite the lack of available money and the health risks of bottle-feeding in poor communities. Fernandez *et al.* (1983, cited in Berry *et al.*, 1992) were able to make a successful intervention to encourage breast-feeding in the Philippines. Their success was based on the behavioural idea of rewards, and they offered women praise, health coupons and lottery tickets as incentives to breast-feed, plant leafy vegetables and visit the health centre every month.

bullying

A modern concern for children's health, although it is probably an old problem, is the experience of **bullying**. Many children experience bullying at school and this may well have an effect on their general health. Natvig *et al.* (2001) surveyed 850 schoolchildren between 13 and 15 in Norway and asked about their general symptoms of health. They found that some symptoms such as such as irritability, headache, backache (boys), and nervousness and sleep disturbance (girls) were more common in children who had some recent experience of bullying (see Table 7.1). It appears that children who experience frequent bullying report substantially more symptoms, some of which might have a long-term negative effect on their health.

• **Table 7.1:** Symptoms and levels of bullying reported by 13–15-year-old schoolchildren

REPORTED SYMPTOM	Victim of bullying last term (all data in %)		
	never n=677	once or twice n=97	sometimes or more n=82
headache	46	46	65
stomach-ache	43	52	70
backache	33	37	55
feeling dizzy	31	26	57
feeling low	39	47	73
irritability	70	73	92
feeling nervous	36	42	55
sleeplessness	41	47	54
AVERAGE FOR ALL SYMPTOMS	**42.4**	**46.3**	**65.1**

the health of older people

The proportion of older people in the European population is higher than it has ever been and it is expected to grow further (Walters *et al.*, 1999). People over 65 made up 9 per cent of the population in the 1950s and are likely to make up 18 per cent of the population in 2020. These figures can be used to spread alarm about the ability of the welfare state to support older people, but what is sometimes overlooked is the level of good health and independence that older people might well enjoy. If our society promotes good health in older people, they will remain fit and active for longer. In the UK, research suggests that physical activity declines sharply at 55 with a third of people over 55 doing no exercise at all, compared with a tenth of people aged 33–54 (Walters *et al.*, 1999). A reasonable target for health promotion, then, is to increase the level of activity in older people.

One of the issues to consider when designing a health promotion for a group of people is that they will have a range of individual needs. Older people are as diverse as any other group in the population – the main feature they share is the length of time they have survived. So if you wanted to promote healthy eating in older people it would not be appropriate to use a simple message like 'reduce the intake of calories and fat' because some older people need to deal with dietary deficiencies. A further health issue for older people is covered in the next chapter on accidents.

CULTURAL DIFFERENCES

traditional societies and health

Horton (1971) described how traditional medical treatments in Africa focus on social factors even when diagnosing infectious diseases. They look for the person who has fallen out with the patient, and who might therefore have 'cast a spell' on them. This seems bizarre to Western minds, yet actually makes perfect sense when the person is seen in a more holistic context.

In a traditional society, with a relatively high rate of infant mortality, those who grow to adulthood tend to have a high natural immunity to disease. So if someone falls sick, the question is not where the germ came from, but how their **immune system** has been weakened to the extent that the illness can take hold. Research suggests that one of the consequences of prolonged stress is to reduce the effectiveness of the immune system. In traditional communities the primary source of stress comes from disturbed interactions with other people. So when the traditional medicine practitioner tries to find out who the person has quarrelled with lately, and to solve their dispute and so lift the spell, this is actually an extremely practical method of treatment. If the stress can be removed then the natural recovery process will be able to fight the illness.

If we applied this approach in a Western setting, we would look for the person at work who is giving you a hard time, or the neighbour who is irritating you beyond belief. However, it is more likely that any medical discussion will involve individual medication rather than social healing.

Theme link to Methodology

Migration: a quasi-experiment

When we carry out an experiment we manipulate an independent variable in order to estimate its effect on one or more other variables. In real life, we are rarely able to make such manipulations. However, sometimes we are able to observe changes and look at them as if we manipulated it. We call this a **quasi-experiment**. An example of this can be seen when people move from one country to another. We can compare the migrants with people from the original culture. For example, the incidence of heart disease in Japan is relatively low, yet Japanese people who moved to the US have the same level of heart disease as other Americans. This shows the influence of culture over health. A further examination of this issue shows that the migrants who took up an American lifestyle had up to five times as many heart problems as the people who kept to the traditional Japanese ways. Interestingly, this difference could not be explained by looking at the traditional risk factors for health such as smoking and diet (Marmot and Syme, 1976).

childbirth pain and culture

A further example of the different descriptions of experience and symptoms comes from cross-cultural studies of childbirth. Taylor (1986) gives a brief summary of these differences and describes how in some cultures, for example Mexico, women have an expectation that childbirth will be painful. The Mexican word for labour (dolor) means *sorrow* or *pain*, in contrast to the English word which means *work*. Taylor suggests that this fearful expectation is followed by painful deliveries with many complications. In contrast, Taylor cites the culture of Yap in the South Pacific where childbirth is treated as an everyday occurrence. Yap women are reported to carry out their normal tasks until they begin labour, at which point they go to a childbirth hut and give birth with the assistance of one or two other women. After the birth, there is a relatively brief rest period before the woman resumes her regular tasks. In this community, complications are reported to be rare. Taylor suggests that expectations are an important factor in the experience of childbirth, and that these expectations come from cultural stories and customs. (Note: I hasten to add that this does not mean that we can reduce the problems and pain of childbirth just by pretending they do not exist.)

GENDER DIFFERENCES IN HEALTH

Men have a lower life expectancy than women: 75.1 years compared with 80.0 years (DoH, 2001b). Men are more likely to die from cancer, heart disease, HIV, accidents and suicide than women (DoH, 1998). Men are more likely to take risks with their health than women – on average they drink more alcohol, smoke more cigarettes, and take more drugs (ONS, 2000). They use less sun cream and are involved in more accidents (DoH, 2001a). Men also have less contact with the health services than women. In response to the question 'Have you consulted your GP in the last two weeks?' 19 per cent of women and only 13 per cent of men said yes. The gender difference was even more pronounced for men under the age of 45 (10 per cent of men compared to 20 per cent of women) (ONS, 1998). Interestingly, other issues of inequality are more pronounced in men than women. In men, social class based on employment is the most important influence on early death. To put it brutally, the less you earn, the sooner you die. For women however, although there is still an effect of income on early death, it is much weaker (Sacker *et al.*, 2000).

The puzzle for health workers is to understand why men have worse health and die younger, and why they make less use of the health services. Recent initiatives by the UK government (Yamey, 2000) have acknowledged that the biggest **health inequality** is between men and women. They are attempting to increase men's involvement in general health promotion such as smoking cessation, and also to deal with specific problems such as prostate cancer. It might be that the problem with men's health is that the area is far less defined than women's health which has a focus around reproductive issues.

Further material on men's health and women's health in covered in the chapters on health promotion and accidents.

Section summary   Psychological research has discovered wide variations in health and health behaviour in different groups in our society. The reasons for these differences are not well understood.

KEY TERMS

bullying
fetal alcohol syndrome
Health Belief Model
health inequality
immune system
laws of magic
lay beliefs
lifestyles
locus of control
mortality
non-rational explanations
optimism
pattern A behaviour
perceived susceptibility
poverty
quasi-experiment
religiosity
self-efficacy

EXERCISE 1

This chapter identifies poverty as a powerful effect in health. Make a list of the factors involved in having a low income that will affect your health. Think about the environmental, social, cognitive, emotional and behavioural features that might have an effect.

Locus of control and self-efficacy are two cognitive explanations of health behaviours. Make a list of brief statements that show you are or are not in control and that you do or do not have self-efficacy. For example, 'whatever I do, I always get sick' (low control), and 'I can reduce my intake of chips and lose 2 pounds in the next two weeks' (high self-efficacy).

ESSAY QUESTION

(a) Describe what psychologists have discovered about how our lifestyle and behavioural choices affect our health.

(b) Discuss the psychological evidence on the effects of lifestyle and behaviour on our health.

(c) Identify a cultural difference in health and suggest one psychological intervention that would be helpful. Give reasons for your answer.

Further reading

You can find an academic review of the various psychological theories of health behaviour in: Conner, M. and Norman, P. (Eds.) (1996) *Predicting health behaviour*. Buckingham: Open University Press.

You might also look at a collection of papers on current issues in health: Heller, T., Muston, R., Sidell, M. and Lloyd, C. (Eds.) (2001) *Working for health*. London: Sage.

Websites

A couple of issues dealt with in the chapter are fetal alcohol syndrome and men's health. You can investigate these on the web by visiting the following:
www.nofas.org
www.menshealthforum.org.uk

Health and safety

Introduction

When we think of accidents, we usually imagine the role of health workers is to pick up the pieces after the accident has occurred. Recently, however, there has been a growing awareness that something can be done to reduce accidents, and that accident reduction is an important part of health promotion. There are several programmes aimed at reducing accidents – for example, reducing falls in older people (DoH, 2000) – and it is an important component of Our Healthier Nation (DoH, 1999, and www.ohn.gov.uk).

THIS CHAPTER LOOKS AT:

- definitions and causes of accidents
- personality and accident proneness
- reducing accidents and promoting safety behaviours.

Definitions, causes and factors affecting accidents

The first issue to consider is what we mean by the term **accident**. A dictionary definition of accidents will have the following elements:

- an event without apparent cause
- an unexpected event
- an unintentional act
- a mishap.

The definition seems quite clear, but there is the little matter of interpretation. One of the problems here concerns the explanations we give for different events. Imagine that you are holding a dinner plate in the kitchen and somehow it ends up smashed on the floor. Your explanation is likely to be 'It slipped out of my hand', or in other words, it was an accident and you could not help it. On the other hand, the explanation of your mother, whose best plate it was, is likely to be 'You dropped it', meaning that it was your fault because of your carelessness, and not an accident at all. You attribute your behaviour to bad luck, and your mother attributes your behaviour to some personal quality.

Psychologists have studied the ways that we make **attributions** like these and have noticed some systematic biases in the way we explain behaviour (for example Hewstone, 1988). For example, we tend to over-estimate the amount of control that someone has over their own behaviour and ignore the way that the situation is affecting them – this is called the *fundamental attribution error*. We tend to blame people rather than circumstance when misfortune occurs near to them. So, is the broken plate the result of an accident or not? Perhaps it's just a matter of interpretation. This digression into the kitchen leaves us with the unresolved question of what is an accident. Instead of trying to resolve it, we will look at the more fruitful area of describing the errors that might lead to accidents.

HUMAN ERROR

One way of categorising **errors** is suggested by Riggio (1990) who identified four types of error that can lead to accidents:

- *Errors of omission*: failing to carry out a task
- *Errors of commission*: making an incorrect action, for example, a health worker giving someone the wrong medicine (see below)
- *Timing errors*: working too quickly, working too slowly
- *Sequence errors*: doing things in the wrong order.

Not all errors lead to accidents and we often make minor errors of judgement without any unfortunate consequences. Sometimes, however, these errors do lead to an event that we call an accident. If we want to reduce accidents, the obvious thing to do is to examine the errors that people most commonly make, and then change the working practices so that the chance of error is reduced. The problem with this is that most workers are reluctant to report errors because of the consequences for them. In the UK there is a legal requirement to report injuries that occur at work, but despite this the Health and Safety Executive estimates that only 47 per cent of non-fatal injuries are reported (HSE, 2001).

Why are accidents under-reported? The problem is that there are often negative consequences for the person involved in the accident and the organisation they work for. The negative consequences to an individual of reporting a personal error or accident include:

- time lost
- feeling guilty
- admitting the mistake
- possible disciplinary action
- possible lost confidence of colleagues
- making a mountain out of molehill.

Another reason why errors and accidents are under-reported is that management often does not want to know about them. The problems for management of receiving an accident report include:

- having a written record of the event which increases the danger of litigation
- increased need for action by management
- increased need for investment in people or equipment
- responsibility is shifted from the worker to the organisation.

What this means is that bad procedures and common errors often go unreported. And if they go unreported and unnoticed then remedial action cannot be taken.

ACCIDENT STATISTICS IN THE UK

road accidents

During 1999 there were just over 235,000 accidents causing personal injury, which caused 320,000 casualties including 3,600 deaths. This actually shows a marked improvement over the last twenty years, as deaths and serious injuries have reduced by 36 per cent and 48 per cent respectively since 1981 (DETR, 1999).

accidents in the home

Around 4,300 people are killed each year in home and garden accidents, and about 170,000 suffered serious injuries that required inpatient treatment in hospital. Home accidents also led to 2.84 million visits to accident and emergency departments.

Some accident figures leave you asking 'why?' and 'how?' For example, according to the Department of Trade and Industry (DTI, 2001), the number of accidents caused by tea cosies is rising (up to 37), though sponge and loofah accidents are in decline (down to 787). They report that the number of people hospitalised after accidents with articles of clothing is 5945 for trouser accidents and 13,132 for socks and tights. It is tempting to fill the rest of the chapter with this data, but I will leave you with the final observation that more people were injured in 1999 from beanbags (1317) than chainsaws (1207). You couldn't make this up.

accidents at work

Surveys indicate that about 1.5 million people each year are hurt at work and treated in casualty departments. Many of the injuries are minor and so are not reported. In 1998/9 there were just under 53,000 major injuries reported, of which 24,000 were to members of the public (RoSPA, 2001a).

All in all, there are millions of accidents each year that require the attention of health workers. Some of these accidents could be avoided, so it is useful to consider the major causes and see what can be done to improve our safety.

CAUSES OF ACCIDENTS

In some respects all accidents are unique, but it is also possible to see some common contributory causes. Reason (2000) says that the problem of human error can be viewed in two ways: the person approach, and the **system approach**. Each way has its own model of the causes of error and suggestions of what is to be done about it. The example below of giving the wrong medicine highlights these two models. The rest of this section will look at some system errors, and the following section will look at the person approach.

the wrong medicine

On the afternoon of January 4th 2001, a day case patient at the Queens Medical Centre (QMC) in Nottingham turned up for his chemotherapy treatment. Under the supervision of a Specialist Registrar, a Senior House Doctor correctly gave the patient a drug (Cytosine) directly into the spine. A second drug (Vincristine) was then also administered by the same route. Unfortunately, this drug should have been given intravenously, and despite the efforts of the medical staff the 19-year-old patient died.

How could this happen? How could two experienced, specialist doctors make what appears to outsiders to be such a basic error? The inquiry into the accident (DoH, 2001d) highlights how professional mistakes (personal causes of error) and the procedures and equipment (system causes) contributed to the death. It was already known that there was a danger of giving Vincristine into the spine because it had happened before. As a result it was part of good practice at the QMC to give the two treatments – one into the spine and one into a vein – on different days, but this procedure was not always followed, especially when patients had a history of missing appointments. Also, the manufacturer of Vincristine provided labels to be attached to the syringes which said 'Not for intrathecal use – For intravenous use only'. However the QMC staff did not use these labels because they believed they had the potential to confuse people. The inquiry also noted that the syringes for both injections looked very similar and that the labels were both in black type.

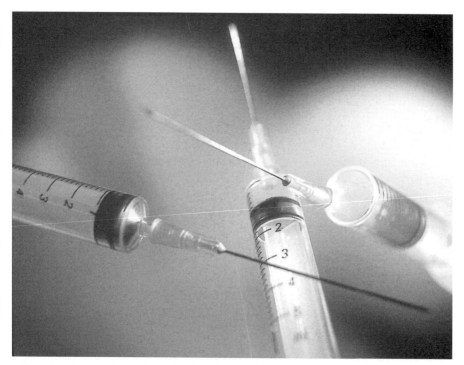

• **Figure 8.1:** Collection of hypodermic syringes with needles attached

Although these system explanations do not explain the accident, they do give some pointers to the ways in which similar mistakes can be avoided. We will go on to look at some examples of how the relationship of people with equipment can lead to accidents.

de-skilling

A source of error in the relationship between operators and machines is the **de-skilling** of the workers. Bainbridge (1987) referred to this as the irony of automation. She pointed out that designers view human operators as unreliable and inefficient, and try to replace them wherever possible with automated devices. Yet this policy often leads directly to an increased number of errors and accidents. The paralysis of the London Ambulance Service, a direct result of the introduction of an automated emergency call routing system in 1993, was a classic example of how this type of problem happens. There are two ironies here: the first is that many mistakes come from the designer's initial errors – systems are introduced which have not been properly worked out and which are actually unable to do what is required of them. Second, as Bainbridge points out, designers still leave people to do the difficult tasks, which cannot be automated so easily.

cognitive overload

The study of **selective attention** highlights some limitations on our ability to process information. An example of this problem was reported by Barber (1988), in a description of an aircraft accident in the area of Zagreb which was then part of Yugoslavia. A British Airways Trident collided with a DC-9 of Inex Adria Airways, resulting in the loss of 176 lives. One of the factors identified as leading to the collision was the cognitive overload of the air traffic controller responsible for the sector the planes were flying in.

At the time of the accident the controller's assistant was missing, there were eleven aircraft in his sector, he was in simultaneous radio communication with four other aircraft, and he was taking part in a telephone conversation with Belgrade concerning two further aircraft. The controller had received very short notice of the arrival of the DC-9 into his sector and it appears that the short notice and the overload of information contributed to the final error. Nevertheless, he was prosecuted and jailed. This is a graphic illustration of the limitations of our information processing capacities, and shows that the public response to disasters is often to blame individuals, when it is the systems within which the individuals are working which are actually at fault.

equipment design

An illustration of the problem of equipment design occurred during World War II (1939–45), and it came about because the US airforce had concentrated on training pilots to fly aircraft rather than designing aircraft that could be flown by pilots. They discovered, however, that even very experienced pilots were prone to make errors with the poorly designed control systems. For example, similar looking controls operating the landing gear and the steering flaps on some B-25 bombers were placed next to each other. The unfortunate consequence of this was that several B-25s were brought into land without the landing gear in place, and so landed on their bellies. The pilots believed that they had activated the landing gear, but in fact they had just steered the plane (Mark, Warm and Huston, 1987). Observations like this have led to the development of aircraft controls that more nearly match the capabilities of pilots.

On a similar theme, some jobs bring their own unique dangers and injuries. For example, football goalkeepers are particularly prone to hand injuries. Most dramatically, there have been a number of injuries caused by the goalkeeper's hand getting caught on the hooks holding up the net. It appears that a ring can get caught up in the netting and the resulting injuries have required amputation of a finger (Scerri and Ratcliffe, 1994). Mind you, the only injury the goalkeeper of my team (Nottingham Forest) gets is backache from picking the ball out of the net.

Accidents are a major cause of injury and death in the UK. Accidents have multiple causes and the explanation we choose to give affects what we do to prevent future hazardous events. If we consider the medical accident at the QMC, perhaps cognitive overload and equipment design were two features that contributed to the fatal mistake. The systems explanation probably provides the most useful approach, but the more popular explanation is to blame the individual.

Personality and accident-proneness

The person approach is the dominant explanation of accidents, especially in medicine (Reason, 2000). Among the advantages of this approach is the satisfying option of naming and blaming people. Individuals are seen as being free agents with the option of choosing between safe and unsafe behaviours. If something goes wrong, it is obvious that it must be the fault of the individual. Taking this view is clearly in the interests of managers and institutions if they want to avoid institutional responsibility.

Early research into industrial accidents tended to focus on individuals, rather than on systems and practices of operation. Greenwood and Woods (1919) performed some of the earliest research into industrial accidents for the Industrial Fatigue Research Board during World War I (1914–19). As part of their study, they explored the idea that some individuals are **accident-prone**, or more likely to have accidents than others. They found statistical distributions of accidents, which seemed to support the idea of accident proneness, and gradually this became accepted as a stable characteristic of certain individuals.

As research developed during the 20th century, the idea of accident-proneness was challenged. Some researchers (for example Arbous and Kerrich, 1951) argued that the initial research had failed to distinguish adequately between the different levels of risk run by people in different jobs. Other researchers performed their own studies and found different outcomes. For example, Adelstein (1952) studied accident rates among railway shunters and found that accidents seemed to occur to anyone and there was no evidence for an accident-prone personality.

Because accidents can occur in all shapes and sizes (tea cosies and cars, for example, as seen above), it seems unlikely that that we can define a single personality type that makes an individual more likely to experience all of them. The way to look at the issues around the personal approach might be to identify the behaviours or personality traits that are most associated with errors and accidents.

REPEATERS

Hill and Trist (1962) investigated **accident repeaters**. While accidents at work may happen to anyone, it is clear that they occur more frequently with some people than with others. Hill and Trist suggested that this might be seen in terms of group norms and compliance – or rather, a refusal to be compliant. On investigating absenteeism and accident rates in a steel works in the early 1950s, they found that strong social norms operated as to which types of absenteeism were acceptable and which were not. Absences which had been certified (for example by a sick note) were regarded as acceptable; unexpected ones and those due to accidents were not. Consequently, the researchers argued, the 'accident repeaters' were actually showing a form of withdrawal from work and a refusal to comply with group norms. It should be noted, though, that an attempted replication of these findings with workers in a photographic process plant failed to produce the same observations (Castle, 1956).

ALCOHOL AND SUBSTANCE ABUSE

The most commonly cited cause of accidents is alcohol or **substance abuse**. When chemicals impair our judgement we are more likely to underestimate the risks of a situation, and overestimate our ability to deal with it. A study of over 500 people attending accident and emergency departments in Scotland examined levels of alcohol (Simpson et al., 2001). About 25 per cent of the attendees showed signs of alcohol. It was especially noticeable in people attending for reasons of self-harm (95 per cent), collapse (47 per cent) assault (50 per cent), and in those who were subsequently admitted to the hospital (50 per cent). These figures suggest that alcohol might well be a factor in a range of accidents that lead to serious injury. A less well researched area is the effect of prescription drugs on performance. Barbone et al. (1998) looked at the medical records of drivers in Scotland involved in their first car accident over a three-year period to identify how many had been prescribed psychoactive drugs such as tranquillisers (for example, benzodiazepines) and antidepressants. There were 19,400 drivers involved in accidents in that period, of which over 1,700 were on some form of psychoactive medication, most commonly benzodiazepines. They concluded that users of benzodiazepines had a 60 per cent higher risk of having a first traffic accident and should be advised not to drive.

LACK OF SLEEP

It is a robust finding from sleep research that **sleep deprivation** affects people so that they (a) make more errors, and (b) need longer to complete a task (Asken, 1983). One particular area of concern is sleep-related vehicle accidents (SRVAs). A substantial survey of 4,600 UK drivers found that 29 per cent admitted to having felt close to falling asleep at the wheel during the previous 12 months (Maycock, 1996). Sleepiness is brought on by long, undemanding, monotonous driving, such as on a motorway. It is also, not surprisingly, affected by the time of day, as our bodily rhythms affect our level of arousal and alertness. One of the problems for drivers who are feeling sleepy is they are often not aware of dropping off for a few seconds. It is a general finding from sleep research that people who are woken within a minute or two of falling asleep commonly deny having been asleep (Horne and Reyner, 1999).

TYPE A BEHAVIOUR PATTERN

One of the personality characteristics that has attracted some attention is the **Type A behaviour pattern** (see Chapter 7). It might be that the time urgency of the Type A pattern leads people into risky situations. The existence of the Type A person is very controversial, though some people believe that the Type A is more disease prone and more likely to have accidents (Suls et al., 1988). There has been some work looking at whether Type A behaviours in drivers increase their accident risk – for example a study of Italian police drivers (Magnavita, 1997) found that drivers with the Type A behaviours had a greater risk of traffic accidents.

An examination of the Type A behaviour pattern raises the question of whether accidents can be reduced by careful personnel selection. Jones and Wuebker (1988) describe how a personnel inventory can be used to predict a number of accident-related events. Using the questionnaire they were able to identify high-risk individuals on the basis of their attitudes and personality, and to place them in less hazardous positions, or send them on special safety training programmes.

INTROVERSION AND EXTROVERSION

Injury data collected over a 12-year period from 171 fire-fighters from a city in the US found that personality traits, including **introversion**, were related to higher injury rates on the job (Liao et al., 2001). They suggested that introverts were less likely to call for assistance, and as fire-fighting requires a high degree of teamwork, it might be that the less integrated and sociable members of the team exposed themselves to greater personal risks. Another finding of the study was that women fire-fighters reported 33 per cent more injuries than their male colleagues, although they returned to work more quickly after injury than the men. The research points to another factor that might contribute to accidents, and that is male culture. They suggested that within groups of male fire-fighters there is a strong cultural norm for not reporting minor injuries because it might be seen as a sign of weakness.

The study of the fire-fighters is particularly interesting because the general view in psychology is that extroversion is the characteristic that is associated with accidents. Extroversion is associated with being impulsive and this has been found to be a feature in people who have car accidents, and accidents at work (Furnham and Heaven, 1999). These apparently contradictory findings illustrate how personality characteristics can interact with the situation someone is in, and the type of task they are asked to carry out, so as to produce an unsafe environment.

AGE

Age is associated with accidents in a number of ways. First, it influences the number and severity of the hazards individuals are exposed to. Second, it is connected to the competence that individuals have at particular tasks, such as crossing the road, and also their skills and attitudes. Children and older people are at the greatest risk of accidents as pedestrians, and they are also at the greatest risk of falls, though for different reasons. In children, the judgement of depth and speed is not fully developed and they may well be unaware of some dangers. For the older person, the problem is limited mobility or failing eyesight. The third problem for the young and old with accidents concerns their ability to respond to and recover from injury (Donaldson and Donaldson, 2000).

PROBLEMS WITH THE PERSON APPROACH

Some accidents can be put down to human error or carelessness or whatever, but many cannot, and following this approach does not offer much advice on how to improve accident rates. Research into quality lapses in the maintenance of aeroplanes found that 90 per cent of them were blameless. If we want to reduce risk, it is important to encourage a culture where errors, slips and near-misses are reported, and a culture where people are named and blamed is not likely to do this. It is believed that the absence of a reporting culture in the Soviet Union contributed to the Chernobyl disaster in 1986. Two explosions blew the 1000-tonne concrete cap off one of the nuclear reactors and released molten core fragments into the surrounding countryside and radioactive material into the atmosphere. This entirely man-made disaster killed more than 30 people at the time, damaged the health of thousands, and contaminated over 400 square miles (Reason, 1990).

Another weakness of the person approach is that two features of human error tend to be overlooked. First, it is often the best people who make the worst mistakes (Reason, 2000). Second, mishaps are not random but tend to occur in patterns. If we go back to the accident at the QMC (see above), then we observe two specialist doctors making a fatal mistake, and this is not the first time that people in that position had made such a mistake. Naming and blaming the doctors is a good course of action if we just want to see people punished for their mistakes, but a bad course of action if we want to stop similar mistakes from happening again.

If we really want to identify the accident-prone person then, on the basis of psychological research, we are looking for a person who tends towards impulsiveness (except in situations that require co-operation), has a sense of time urgency, has taken alcohol (and possibly benzodiazepines) recently. He or she is not happy at their job, is a bit short of sleep and is either a child or a retired person. This is everyone and no-one, so it is probably not very useful to try and identify a type of person who is accident-prone.

Section summary

The person approach to accidents is satisfying but flawed. It has not been possible to identify an accident-prone type of person, but there is some evidence about the characteristics and behaviour patterns that make people more likely to have accidents or make errors.

Reducing accidents and promoting safety behaviours

ACCIDENT REDUCTION AT WORK

Health promotion can be used at work to reduce accidents. The most frequently cited methods for reducing accidents at work are **stress reduction** programmes. For example, Kunz (1987) describes how a stress intervention programme reduced medical costs and accident claims in a hospital. The programme more than paid for itself with the savings from reduction in accidents. Stress reduction programmes have also been shown to reduce absenteeism (Murphy and Sorenson, 1988).

Another way of reducing accidents is through incentive programmes. Fox et al. (1987) looked at the effects of a token economy programme at open cast pits. Employees earned stamps for working without time lost for injuries, for being in work groups in which none of the workers had lost time through injury, for not being involved in equipment damaging accidents, for making safety suggestions, and for behaviour that prevented injury or accident. They lost stamps for equipment damage, injuries to their work group and failure to report accidents and injuries. The token economy produced a dramatic reduction in days lost through injury and reduced the costs of accidents and injuries. These improvements were maintained over a number of years.

A relatively simple intervention to reduce fatigue and accidents in logging workers involved encouraging them to take regular fluids. Sports science has shown that the use of regular fluid intake is one way to reduce the sense of strain in a task and delay the onset of physical and mental fatigue. A study of loggers in New Zealand (Paterson et al., 1998) looked at the normal performance of the loggers and compared it with performance when they were taking a sports drink every 15 minutes. In the normal condition, the loggers lost on average about 1 per cent of their body weight during the working day, but in the fluid condition they maintained or increased their body weight. Also in the fluid condition, the heart rate was lower, and the loggers reported feeling fresher, stronger, more alert and more vigorous. Reducing fatigue and strain can reduce errors so it is a useful intervention to keep a worker properly hydrated.

Other methods of reducing accidents at work include *poster campaigns* to raise awareness of hazards and encourage a realistic assessment of risk, *staff training* and *organisational review*.

MEDIA CAMPAIGNS

Public information films on television often tell us to do very sensible things like dip our headlights or fit smoke alarms. They might well affect our **attitudes** to these procedures and products but do they affect our behaviour? In the field of accidents it is possible to estimate changes in behaviour by comparing accident rates before and after an advertising campaign. This discrepancy between attitude (what we think) and behaviour (what we do) is illustrated in a report by Cowpe (1989). This report looked at the effectiveness of a series of advertisements about the dangers of chip pan fires. Before the advertisements, people were asked about this hazard and most of them claimed that they always adopted safe practices. However, the statistics from fire brigades about the frequency of chip pan fires and the descriptions by people of what they should do suggested that their behaviour was not as safe as they thought. A television advertising campaign was developed and broadcast showing dramatic images of exactly how these fires develop, and how people should deal with them. The adverts ended with a simple statement, such as 'Of course, if you don't overfill your chip pan in the first place, you won't have to do any of this'.

By comparing fire brigade statistics for the areas which received the advertisements, and those for the areas which did not, the advertisers found that the advertisements had produced a 25 per cent reduction in the number of chip pan fires in some areas, with a 12 per cent reduction overall (see Figure 8.2). Surveys taken after the series of advertisements showed that people had more accurate knowledge about what they should do in the event of a chip pan fire than before. The implication from this report is very clear. Public information films and health promotion advertisements are most effective if they contain information about what to do rather than what to think or what to be scared of.

SLEEPY DRIVERS

As mentioned above, there is a problem in the UK with sleep-related vehicle accidents (SRVAs). There has been extensive research into this issue (Reyner and Horn, 1998) which shows that the methods suggested to prevent this by motoring organisations, such as opening the window or turning up the radio,

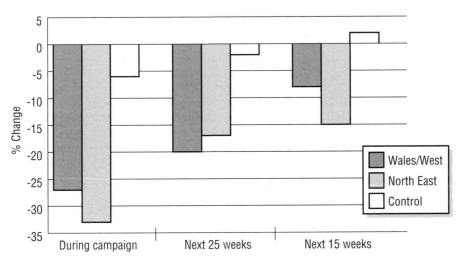

• **Figure 8.2:** Change in the number of chip pan fires during and immediately after the advertising campaign in two television regions

only have small and short-term benefits (about 15 minutes). The best advice is to take a break and maybe have a nap. It has been found that naps of between 4 and 20 minutes can have a positive effect on performance and reduce sleepiness. In fact, 15-minute naps taken every 6 hours during a period of 35 hours of no sleep have been found to be effective in maintaining a good level of performance. The common technique of having some coffee is also a good one, and laboratory tests have shown that low doses of caffeine (100–200 mg, or about two cups of coffee) improve alertness in sleepy people. The answer is fairly clear. To reduce road SRVAs we need to encourage drivers to stop driving when sleepy, and to take a nap or drink some coffee (for a review see Horn and Reyner, 1999).

MOBILE PHONES

There is concern about the use of mobile phones by drivers (and by passengers on trains – Ed). A review of research by RoSPA (RoSPA, 2001b) about the effects of using mobile phones on driving found that when the driver is using a hand-held or hands-free phone they (a) vary their road speed and (b) wander in their lane. The driver appears to lose touch with driving conditions and become distracted. They concluded that using a mobile phone when driving increases the risk of having an accident. Interestingly, not all research paints such a negative picture of the phone user. For example Alm (1998) tested the idea that the more demanding the driving task, the greater would be the effect on using a mobile phone. The study did not support the hypothesis and showed, in fact, that drivers under pressure of a demanding road will reduce the level of difficulty by, for example slowing down, when they are using a mobile phone. This suggests that we are able to successfully multi-task and adjust our behaviour to match the actions we are required to do.

The health promotion strategy to reduce accidents in drivers who are using mobile phones is carried out though driver education, through legislation (drivers must be in proper control of their vehicles at all times), and through employer education (so that they do not require their drivers to be available on the phone at all times).

PREVENTING SLIPS, TRIPS AND FALLS

Slips, trips and falls make up around a third of injuries leading to absence from work (HSE, 1999). Older people are especially susceptible to health-damaging falls, with approximately 30 per cent of people over 65 who live in the community falling each year and about 50 per cent of the over 80s (DoH, 2000). The consequences of falling can be:

- physical injury such as fractures
- psychological impacts such as increased fear of falling
- reduced mobility
- needing to be cared for in an institution
- death.

There have been many programmes aimed at reducing damaging falls in older people. Studies that have targeted high-risk groups and offered programmes of exercise aimed at increasing mobility and strength have been relatively ineffective in reducing the number of falls. Programmes which have the greatest success combine a number of interventions such as a review of the medication the older person is taking, a safety review of their house and taking moderate exercise (for a review see DoH, 2000). For people at particular risk, there have been some interventions using hip protection so that falls are cushioned and less damaging. The problem with such interventions is that the compliance rate for wearing the devices is relatively low.

UNDERSTANDING MEDICAL INSTRUCTIONS

We live in a world full of icons and signs. Diagrams of stick people with crosses through them appear all over our everyday environment. What is the stick figure doing? Does everybody understand the same message from these signs? Research into signs can help us adjust them so that more people can understand what is required and make less errors in medication. For example, a study by Dowse and Ehlers (1998) on the different perceptions of signs by black and white people in South Africa, was able to devise signs that could be better recognised by the black community. Literacy in the black community is still very low in South Africa (estimated 45 per cent illiterate and 25 per cent semi-literate), so the use of icons and pictures is important in medical instructions. A set of international symbols was published in 1991 in the United States Pharmacopoeia, but the researchers believed that many of these symbols would be poorly understood by black South Africans. Following interviews with black students they devised some Africanised versions of the symbols (see Figure 8.3). When they tested them with members of their target group (black South Africans with low levels of literacy), they found that the Africanised symbols were either equally well or better recognised than the US symbols.

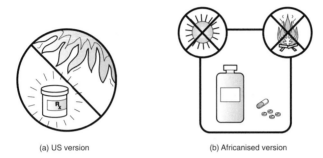

(a) US version   (b) Africanised version

Figure 1 'Do not store near heat or sunlight'

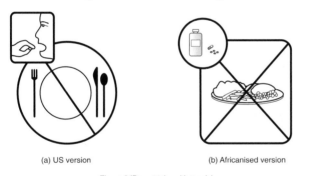

(a) US version   (b) Africanised version

Figure 2 'Do not take with meals'

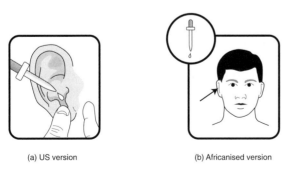

(a) US version   (b) Africanised version

Figure 3 'Place drops in the ear'

• **Figure 8.3:** US and Africanised symbols for medical instructions, adapted from Dowse and Ehlers (1998)

Section summary Preventing accidents is easier said than done. Attempts to improve the safety of the environment and to improve good practice at work can help to reduce the frequency of damaging errors.

KEY TERMS

accident
accident-prone
accident repeaters
attitudes
attributions
de-skilling
errors
introversion
selective attention
sleep deprivation
stress reduction
substance abuse
system approach
type A behaviour pattern

EXERCISE **1**

Find a tea cosy (you will probably have to go round to your gran's) and examine it carefully. Make a list of improvements in the design so that we can reduce the number of accidents requiring hospital treatment.

EXERCISE **2**

Look around your home and identify the number of possible hazards. What can you do to reduce the risk of accident? Careful – this might end up with you cleaning the place up, and this has hazards of its own, such as a bad back.

(a) Describe what psychologists have discovered about accidents.

(b) Discuss the psychological evidence on accidents.

(c) Suggest a psychological intervention that would be helpful in reducing accidents from the use of tea cosies in the home. Give reasons for your answer.

Further reading

If you want to read a general psychological text on accidents and errors then look no further than: Reason, J. (1990) *Human error*. Cambridge: Cambridge University Press. On the other hand if you want to read a detailed account of the medical accident at the Queens Medical Centre described above then you can get it from the Department of Health or go to: www.doh.gov.uk/qmcinquiry/index.htm.

Websites

The Royal Society for the Prevention of Accidents is a registered charity which was established over 80 years ago. Providing information, advice, resources and training, RoSPA is actively involved in the promotion of safety in all areas of life – at work, in the home, and on the roads, in schools, at leisure and on or near water. RoSPA aims to campaign for change, influence opinion, contribute to debate, educate and inform: www.rospa.co.uk

The Health and Safety Executive (HSE) say that their mission is 'To ensure that risks to people's health and safety from work activities are properly controlled.' My mission, on the other hand, is to finally finish this text on looking after our health and then leg it to the pub. www.hse.gov.uk

References

Abel, E. L. (1998) Prevention of alcohol abuse-related birth effects, II. Targeting and pricing. *Alcohol and Alcoholism,* 33(4), 417–420.

Abraham, C., Costa-Pereira, A., Du-V-Florey, C. & Ogston, S. (1999) Cognitions associated with initial medical consultations concerning recurrent breathing difficulties: A community based sample. *Psychology and Health,* 14(5), 913–925.

Abraham, S. C. S., Sheeran, P., Spears, R. & Abrams, D. (1992) Health beliefs and the promotion of HIV-preventive intentions among teenagers: A Scottish perspective. *Health Psychology,* 11, 363–370.

Adams, J. H., Aubert, R. E. & Clark, V. R. (1999) The relationship between John Henryism, hostility, perceived stress, social support, and blood pressure in African-American college students. *Ethnicity and Disease,* 9(3), 359–368.

Adelstein, A. M. (1952) Accident proneness: a criticism of the concept based on an analysis of shunters' accidents. *Journal of the Royal Statistical Society,* 115, 111–118.

Alm, H. (1998) Traffic safety and mobile phones. In P. A. Scott, R. S. Bridger & J. Charteris (Eds.), *Global Ergonomics* (pp. 181-184). Oxford: Elsevier.

Als, A. B. (1997) The desk-top computer as a magic box: Patterns of behaviour connected with the desk-top computer; GP's and patients' perceptions. *Family Practice,* 14(1), 17–23.

Arbous, A. G. & Kerrich, J. E. (1951) Accident statistics and the concept of accident proneness. *Biometrics,* 7, 340–429.

Argyle, M. (1975) *Bodily communication.* London: Methuen.

Armitage, C. J. & Conner, M. (2000) Social cognition models and health behaviour: a structured review. *Psychology and Health,* 15(2), 173–189.

Asch, S. E. (1955) Opinions and Social Pressure. *Scientific American,* 193, 31–35.

Ashton, H. & Golding, J. F. (1989) Smoking: motivation and models. In T. Ney & A. Gale (Eds.), *Smoking and Human Behaviour* (pp. 21–56). Chichester: Wiley.

Ashton, L., Karnilowicz, W. & Fooks, D. (2001) The incidence and belief structures associated with breast self-examination. *Social Behavior and Personality,* 29(3), 223–229.

Asken, M. & Raham, D. (1983) Resident performance and sleep deprivation: A review. *Journal of Medical Education,* 58, 382–388.

Association, A. P. (1994) *Diagnostic and Statistical Manual IV.* Washington, USA: APA.

Bachman, J. G., Johnson, L. D., O'Malley, P. M. & Humphreys, H. (1988) Explaining the recent decline in marijuana use: differentiating the effects of perceived risks, disapproval, and general life-style factors. *Journal of Health and Social Behaviour,* 29, 92–112.

Bader, S. A. & Braude, R. M. (1998) 'Patient informatics': Creating new partnerships in medical decision making. *Academic Medicine,* 73(4), 408–411.

Baillie, C., Smith, J., Hewison, J. & Mason, G. (2000) Ultrasound screening for chromosomal abnormality: women's reactions to false positive results. *British Journal of Health Psychology,* 5(4), 377–394.

Bainbridge, L. (1987) The ironies of automation. In J. Rasmussen, K. Duncan & J. Leplat (Eds.) *New Technology and Human Error.* London: Wiley.

Balding, J. W. (2001) The Health Related Behaviour Questionnaire. *Education and Health,* 18(3), 57–60.

Bandura, A. (1977) Self-efficacy. *Psychological Review,* 84, 191–215.

Barat, I., Andreasen, F. & Damsgaard, E. M. (2001) Drug therapy in the elderly: what doctors believe and patients actually do. *British Journal of Clinical Pharmacology,* 51(6), 615–622.

Barber, P. (1988) *Applied Cognitive Psychology.* New York: Routledge.

Barbone, F., McMahon, A. D., Davet, P. G., Morris, A. D., Reid, I. C., McDevitt, D. G. & MacDonald, T. M. (1998) Association of road-traffic accidents with benzodiazepine use. *The Lancet,* 352(9137), 1331–1336.

Basler, H. D. & Rehfisch, H. P. (1990) Follow-up results of a cognitive–behavioural treatment for chronic pain in a primary care setting. *Psychology and Health,* 4, 293–304.

Becker, M. H. & Rosenstock, I. M. (1984) Compliance with medical advice. In A. Steptoe & A. Mathews (Eds.), *Health Care and Human Behaviour.* London: Academic Press.

Beckman, H. B. & Frankel, R. M. (1984) The effect of physician behavior on the collection of data. *Annals of International Medicine,* 101, 692–696.

Benbassat, J., Pilpel, D. & Tidhar, M. (1998) Patients' preferences for participation in clinical decision-making: A review of published studies. *Behavioral Medicine,* 24, 81–88.

Bernstein, L., Garzone, P. D., Rudy, T., Kramer, B., Stiff, D. & Peitzman, A. (1995) Pain perception and serum beta-endorphin in trauma patients. *Psychosomatics,* 36(3), 276–284.

Berry, J., Pootinga, Y. H., Segall, M. H. & Dasen, P. R. (1992) *Cross-cultural psychology*. Cambridge: Cambridge University Press.

Blanchard, C. G., Labrecque, M. S., Ruckdeschel, J. C. & Blanchard, E. B. (1988). Information and decision-making preferences of hospitalized cancer patients. *Social Science and Medicine, 27*, 1139–1148.

Bowlby, J. (1969) *Attachment and Loss, Vol 1: Attachment, 2nd ed.* London: The Hogarth Press.

Boyle, C. M. (1970) Differences between patients' and doctors' interpretations of common medical terms. *British Medical Journal, 2*, 286–289.

Breslow, L. & Enstrom, J. (1980) Persistance of medical habits and their relationship to mortality. *Preventive Medicine, 9*, 469–483.

Bridge, L. R., Benson, P., Pietroni, P. C. & Priest, R. G. (1988) Relaxation and imagery in the treatment of breast cancer. *British Medical Journal, 297*, 1169–1172.

British Psychological Society, T. (1993) *Response to The Health of the Nation*. Leicester: The British Psychological Society.

Brown, G. W. & Harris, T. O. (1989) *Life Events and Illness*. London: Unwin Hyman.

Budzynski, T. H., Stovya, J. & Adler, C. S. (1970) Feedback-induced muscle relaxation: Application to tension headache. *Journal of Behaviour Therapy and Experimental Psychiatry, 1*, 205–211.

Bunker, J. P. (2001) Ivan Illich and the pursuit of health. In T. Heller, R. Muston, M. Sidell & C. Lloyd (Eds.), *Working for Health* (pp. 43–53). London: Sage.

Carroll, D., Davey Smith, G. & Bennett, P. (1994) Health and socio-economic status. *The Psychologist, 7*, 122–125.

Castle, P. F. C. (1956) Accidents, absence and withdrawal from the work situation. *Human Relations, 9*, 223–233.

Chery Croze, S. & Duclaux, R. (1980).Discrimination of painful stimuli in human beings. *Journal of Neurophysiology, 44*, 1–10.

Chung, K. F. & Naya, I. (2000) Compliance with an oral asthma medication: a pilot study using an electronic monitoring device. *Respiratory Medicine, 94*(9), 852–858.

Clark, K. M., Friedman, H. & Martin, L. R. (1999). A longitudinal study of religiosity and mortality risk. *Journal of Health Psychology, 4*(3), 381–391.

Cluss, P. A. & Epstein, L. H. (1985) The measurement of medical compliance in the measurement of disease. In P. Karoly (Ed.) *Measurement Strategies in Health Psychology*. New York: Wiley.

Cohen, S., Kamarck, T. & Mermelstein, R. (1983) A global measure of perceived stress. *Journal of Health and Social Behavior, 24*, 385–396.

Comings, D. E. (1998) The molecular genetics of pathological gambling. *CNS Spectrums, 3*(6), 20–37.

Cowpe, C. (1989) Chip pan fire prevention: 1976–1984. In C. Channon (Ed.), *Twenty Advertising Case Histories (2nd series)*. London: Cassell.

Day, J. J., Bayer, A. A., Pathy, M. S. & Chadha, J. S. (1987) Acute myocardial infraction: diagnostic difficulties and outcomes in advanced old age. *Age and Ageing,* 16, 239–247.

Department for Education and Employment (1997) *Excellence in Schools.* London: HMSO.

Department of Health (1992) *The Health Of The Nation: A Strategy for Health in England.* London: HMSO.

Department of Health (1993a) *The Effect of Tobacco Advertising on Tobacco Consumption.* London: Economics and Operational Research Division.

Department of Health (1993b) *Working Together for Better Health.* London: HMSO.

Department of Health (1998) *Inequalities in health.* London: HMSO.

Department of Health (1999) *Saving Lives: Our Healthier Nation:* HMSO.

Department of Health (2000) *Guidelines for the prevention of falls in older people:* HMSO.

Department of Health (2001a) *Health Survey for England: The health of ethnic minority groups 1999:* HMSO.

Department of Health (2001b) *Health and Personal Social Services Statistics,* [world wide web]. Government Statistical Service [2001, 02/08/01].

Department of Health (2001c) Statistics on alcohol: England, 1978 onwards. *Statistical Bulletin,* 13.

Department of Health (2001d) *External inquiry into the adverse incident that occurred at Queen's Medical Centre, Nottingham, 4th January 2001.* London: DoH.

Department of the Environment, T. a. t. R. (1999) *Road accidents in Great Britain: 1999 The casualty report.* London: HMSO.

Department of Trade and Industry (2001) *Home and Leisure Accident Surveillance System.* London: HMSO.

Diamond, E. G., Kittle, C. F. & Crockett, J. F. (1960) Comparison of internal mammary artery ligation and sham operation for angina pectoris. *American Journal of Cardiology,* 5, 483–486.

Dijkstra, A. & De Vries, H. (2001) Do self-help interventions in health education lead to cognitive changes, and do cognitive changes lead to behavioural changes? *British Journal of Health Psychology,* 6(2), 121–134.

DiMatteo, M. R. & DiNicola, D. D. (1982) *Achieving Patient Compliance: The psychology of the medical practitioner's role.* New York: Pergamon Press.

Donaldson, L. J. & Donalson, R. J. (2000) *Essential Public Health.* (2nd ed.). Newbury, UK: Petroc Press.

Dorling, D., Mitchell, R., Shaw, M., Orford, S. & Smith, G. D. (2000) The ghost of Christmas past: health effects of poverty in London in 1896 and 1991. *British Medical Journal,* 321, 1547–1551.

Dorling, D., Smith, G. D. & Shaw, M. (2001) Analysis of trends in premature mortality by Labour voting in the 1997 general election. *British Medical*

Journal, 322, 1336–1337.

Douglas, R. B., Blanks, R., Crowther, A. & Scott, G. (1988) A study of stress in West Midlands firemen, using ambulatory electrocardiograms.Special Issue: Stress in the public services. *Work and Stress,* 2, 309–318.

Dowse, R. & Ehlers, M. S. (1998) The development and evaluation of pharmaceutical pictograms. In P. A. Scott, R. S. Bridger, & J. Charteris (Eds.), *Global Ergonomics* (pp. 565–570). Oxford: Elsevier.

Dressler, W. W., Bindon, J. R. & Neggers, Y. H. (1998) John Henryism, gender and arterial blood pressure in an African American community. *Psychosomatic Medicine,* 60(5), 620–624.

Dryden, W. (1996) Rational Emotive Behaviour Therapy. In W. Dryden (Ed.), *Handbook of Individual Therapies* (pp. 304–327). London: Sage.

Dumas, R. M. (1994) Early memory loss occurs when offspring's mother exposed to alcohol. *Neurotoxicology and Teratology,* 166, 605–612.

Edelmann, R. J. (2000) *Psychosocial Aspects of the Health Care Process.* Harlow, UK: Prentice Hall.

Erskine, A. & Williams, A. C. (1989) Chronic pain. In A. K. Broome (Ed.), *Health Psychology: Processes and applications.* London: Chapman and Hall.

Eysenbach, G. & Diepgen, T. L. (1998) Evaluation of cyberdocs. *The Lancet,* 352, 1526.

Eysenbach, G., Ryoung Sa, E. & Diepgen, T. I. (2001) Towards the millennium of cybermedicine. In T. Heller, R. Muston, M. Sidell, & C. Lloyd (Eds.), *Working for Health* (pp. 351–357). London: Sage.

Ezzo, J., Berman, B., Hadhazy, V. A., Jadad, A. R., Lao, L. & Singh, B. B. (2000) Is acupuncture effective for the treatment of chronic pain? A systematic review. *Pain,* 86(3), 217–225.

Farquhar, J. W., Maccoby, N., Wood, P. D., Alexander, J. K. *et al.* (1977) Community education for cardiovascular health. *The Lancet,* 1192–1195.

Feurstein, M., Labbé, E. & Kuczmeirczyk, A. (1986) *Health Psychology: A psychobiological perspective.* New York: Plenum.

Fitzpatrick, J. & Dollamore, G. (1999) Examining adult mortality rates using the National Statistics for Socio-Economic Classification. *Health Statistics Quarterly,* 2, 33–40.

Forsythe, M., Calnan, M. & Wall, B. (1999) Doctors as patients: postal survey examining consultants and general practitioners adherence to guidelines. *British Medical Journal,* 319, 605–608.

Fox, D., Hopkins, B. & Anger, W. (1987) The long-term effects of a token economy on safety performance in open-pit mining. *Journal of Applied Behaviour Analysis,* 20, 215–224.

Fraser, S., Bunce, C., Wormald, R. & Brunner, E. (2001) Deprivation and late presentation of glaucoma: case control study. *British Medical Journal* (322).

Friedman, M. & Rosenman, R. H. (1959) Association of specific overt behaviour pattern with blood cardiovascular findings. *Journal of American*

Medical Association, 169, 1286–1296.

Friedman, M. & Rosenman, R. H. (1974) *Type A behaviour and your heart.* New York: Alfred A. Knopf.

Furnham, A. & Heaven, P. (1999) *Personality and Social Behaviour.* London: Arnold.

Goldberg, D. (1978) *A User's Guide to the General Health Questionnaire.* Windsor: NFER-Nelson.

Gomel, M., Oldenburg, B., Lemon, J., Owen, N. & Westbrook, F. (1993) Pilot study of the effects of workplace smoking bans on indices of smoking, cigarette craving, stress and other health behaviours. *Psychology and Health,* 8, 223–29.

Greatbatch, D., Heath, C., Campion, P. & Luff, P. (1995) How do desk-top computers affect the doctor–patient interaction? *Family Practice,* 12, 1, 32–36.

Greenwood, M. & Woods, H. M. (1919) The incidence of industrial accidents upon individuals with special reference to multiple accidents, *Industrial Health Research Board Report no. 4* . London: HMSO.

Griffiths, M. D. (1995) *Adolescent Gambling.* London: Routledge.

Grohol, J. M. (1998) Future clinical directions: Professional Development, Pathology and Psychologtherapy on-line. In J. Gackenbach (Ed.), *Psychology of the Internet* (pp. 111–138). New York: Academic Press.

Gulian, E., Glendon, A. I., Matthews, G. & Davies, D. *et al.* (1990) The stress of driving: A diary study. *Work and Stress,* 4, 7–16.

Han, C., McGue, M. K. & Iacono, W. G. (1999) Lifetime tobacco, alcohol and other substance use in adolescent Minnesota twins: univariate and multivariate behavioral genetic analyses. *Addiction,* 94, 7, 981–993.

Harden, A., Peersman, G., Oliver, S., Mauthner, M. & Oakley, A. (1999) A systematic review of the effectiveness of health promotion interventions in the workplace. *Occupational Medicine,* 49, 8, 540–548.

Harkness, S., Wyon, J. & Super, C. (1988) The relevance of behavioural sciences to disease prevention and control in developing countries. In P. Dasen, J. Berry & N. Sartorius (Eds.), *Cross-cultural psychology and health: Towards applications.* London: Sage.

Harris, D. M. & Gluten, S. (1979) Health-protective behaviour: An exploratory study. *Journal of Health and Social Behaviour,* 20, 17–29.

Health and Safety Executive. (2001) *Safety Statistics Bulletin 2000/1.* London: HSE.

Health and Saftey Executive. (1999b) *Slips and Trips: Guidance for employers on identifying hazards and controlling risks* (HS(G) 155). Sudbury: HSE.

Heather, N. (1994) Weakness of will: a suitable topic for scientific study? *Addiction Research,* 2, 135–139.

Heller, T., Muston, R., Sidell, M. & Lloyd, C. (Eds.) (2001) *Working for Health.* London: Sage.

Hewstone, M., Stroebe, W., Codol, J. P. & Stephenson, G. (1988) *Introduction to Social Psychology: A European Perspective*. Oxford: Blackwell.

Hill, J. M. M. & Trist, E. L. (1972) Industrial accidents, sickness and other absences, *Tavistock Pamphlet no. 4* . London: Tavistock.

Holmes, T. H. & Rahe, R. H. (1967) The Social Readjustment Rating Scale. *Journal of Psychosomatic Research,* 11, 213–218.

Horn, S. & Munafò, M. (1997) *Pain: Theory, research and intervention*. Buckingham UK: Open University Press.

Horne, J. & Reyner, L. (1999) Vehicle accidents related to sleep: a review. *Occupational and Environmental Medicine,* 56, 289–294.

Horton, R. (1971) African traditional thought and Western science. In M. F. D. Young (Ed.), *Knowledge and Control* . Cambridge, MA. Addison-Wesley.

Howlett, D., Rushforth, A. & Stevens, D. (2000). Parents do not always understand things doctors might say to them. *British Medical Journal,* 321, 1160.

Humphreys, R. (2001) *The Rough Guide to London*. London: Rough Guides.

Illich, I. (1975) *Medical Nemesis: The expropriation of health*. London: Calder & Boyars.

Impicciatore, P., Pandolfini, C., Casella, N. & Bonati, M. (1997) Reliability of health information for the public on the world wide web: systematic survey of advice on managing fever in children at home. *British Medical Journal,* 314, 1875–1881.

Jackson, L. A. & Adams-Campbell, L. L. (1994) John Henryism and blood pressure in black college students. *Journal of Behavioral Medicine, 17*(1), 69–79.

James, S. A., Strogatz, D. S., Wing, S. B. & Ramsey, D. L. (1987) Socioeconomic status, John Henryism, and hypertension in blacks and whites. *American Journal of Epidemiology,* 126, 664–673.

Jamner, L. D. & Tursky, B. (1987) Syndrome-specific descriptor profiling: A psychophysiological and psychophysical approach. *Health Psychology,* 6, 417–430.

Jang, K. L., Vernon, P. A. & Livesley, W. J. (2000) Personality disorder traits, family environment and alcohol misuse: a multivariate behavioural genetic analysis. *Addiction, 95*, 6, 873–888.

Janis, I. & Feshbach, S. (1953) Effects of fear-arousing communications. *Journal of Abnormal and Social Psychology,* 48, 78–92.

Johnson, J. & Bytheway, B. (2001) The use of medicines bought in pharmacies and other retail outlets. In T. Heller, R. Muston, M. Sidell & C. Lloyd (Eds.) *Working for Health* (pp. 319–328). London: Sage.

Joinson, A. N. (1998) Causes and implications of disinhibited behaviour on the Net. In J. Gackenbach (Ed.) *Psychology of the Internet* (pp. 43–60). New York: Academic Press.

Jones, J. & Wuebker, L. (1988) Accident prevention through personnel selection. *Journal of Business and Psychology, 3,* 187–198.

Kahn, G. S. (1997) Digital interactive media and the health care balance of power. In R. L. Street, W. R. Gold, & T. R. Manning (Eds.) *Health promotion and interactive technology: Theoretical applications and future directions* (pp. 187–208). NJ, USA: Lawrence Earlbaum Associates.

Kanner, A. D., Coynes, J. C., Schaefer, C. & Lazarus, R. S. (1981) Comparison of two modes of stress measurement: daily hassles and uplifts versus major life events. *Journal of Behavioural Medicine, 4,* 1–39.

Kanter, J. & Streissguth, A. P. (Eds.) (1997) *The challenge of fetal alcohol syndrome – overcoming secondary disabilities.* Washington: University of Washington Press.

Kaplan, R. M., Sallis, J. F. & Patterson, T. L. (1993) *Health and Human Behaviour.* New York: McGraw-Hill.

Karoly, P. (1985a) The assessment of pain: concepts and procedures. In P. Karoly (Ed.) *Measurement Strategies in Health Psychology.* New York: Wiley.

Karoly, P. (1985b) *Measurement Strategies in Health Psychology.* New York: Wiley.

Klesges, R. C., Vasey, B. S. & Glasgow, R. E. (1986) A worksite smoking modification competition: potential for public health impact. *American Journal of Public Health, 76,* 198–200.

Kline, K. N. & Mattson, M. (2000) Breast self-examination pamphlets: a content analysis grounded in fear appeals research. *Health Communication, 12,* 1, 1–21.

Kobasa, S. C. (1979) Stressful life events, personality and health: An inquiry into hardiness. *Journal of Personality and Social Psychology, 37,* 1–11.

Korsch, B. M., Gozzi, E. K. & Francis, V. (1968) Gaps in doctor–patient communication. *Pediatrics, 42,* 855–871.

Kotzer, A. M. & Foster, R. (2000) Children's use of PCA following spinal fusion. *Orthopedic Nursing, 19,* 5, 19–27.

Kunz, L. (1987) Stress intervention programs for reducing medical costs and accident claims in a hospital. *Journal of Business and Psychology, 1,* 257–263.

Lazarus, R. & Folkman, S. (1984) *Stress, Appraisal and Coping.* New York: Springer.

Leenaars, P. E. M., Rombouts, R. & Kok, G. (1993) Seeking medical care for a sexually transmitted disease: Determinants of delay-behavior. *Psychology and Health, 8,* 17–32.

Leng, G. (1999) A year of acupuncture in palliative care. *Palliative Medicine, 13,* 2, 163–164.

Ley, P. (1979) Memory for medical information. *British Journal of Social and Clinical Psychology, 18,* 245–255.

Ley, P. (1988) *Communicating with Patients.* London: Croom Helm.

Ley, P. (1989) Improving patients' understanding, recall, satisfaction and compliance. In A. K. Broome (Ed.) *Health Psychology: Processes and Applications*. London: Chapman and Hall.

Ley, P., Bradshaw, P. W., Eaves, D. & Walker, C. M. (1973) A method for increasing patients' recall of information presented by doctors. *Psychological Medicine,* 3, 217–220.

Liao, H., Arvey, R. D. & Butler, R. J. (2001) Correlayes of work frequency and duration among firefighters. *Journal of Occupationsl Health Psychology,* 6(3).

Lindeman, M., Keskivaara, P. & Roschier, M. (2000) Assessment of magical beliefs about food and health. *Journal of Health Psychology,* 5(2), 195–209.

Loeser, J. D. & Melzack, R. (1999). Pain: an overview. *The Lancet, 353,* 1607–1609.

Macleod, U., Ross, S., Twelves, C., George, W. D., Gillis, C. & Watt, G. C. M. (2000) Primary and secondary care management of women with earlt breast cancer from affluent and deprived areas: retorspective review of hospital and general practice records. *British Medical Journal,* 320, 1442–1445.

MacReady, N. (2000) Myocardial infraction: changing view of a killer. *The Lancet,* 356, 572.

Magnavita, N., Narda, R., Sani, L., Carbone, A., De Lorenzo, G. & Sacco, A. (1997) Type A behaviour pattern and traffic accidents. *British Journal of Medical Psychology, 70*(1), 103–107.

Mark, L. S., Warm, J. S. & Huston, R. L. (1987) *Ergonomics and human factors: Recent research*. New York: Springer-Verlag.

Marmot, M. G. & Syme, S. L. (1976) Acculturation and coronary heart disease in Japanese-Americans. *American Journal of Epidemiology,* 104, 225–247.

Marteau, T. M. (1990) Framing of information: Its influence upon decisions of doctors and patients, *Proceedings of the Second conference of the Health Psychology Section. BPS Occasional Papers No. 2.* Leicester: British Psychological Society.

Marteau, T. M. (1993) Health-related screening: psychological predictors of uptake and impact. In S. Maes, H. Leventhal & M. Johnston (Eds.) *International Review of Psychology Vol. II*. Chichester: Wiley.

Matarazzo, J. D. (1982) Behavioral health's challenge to academic, scientific, and professional psychology. *American Psychologist,* 37, 1–14.

Maycock, G. (1996) Sleepiness and driving: the experience of UK drivers. *Journal of Sleep Research,* 5, 229–237.

McDonald, A. J. & Cooper, M. G. (2001) Patient-controlled analgesia: an appropriate method of pain control in children. *Paediatric Drugs, 2001*(3), 4.

McGowan, L. P. A., Clarke-Carter, D. D. & Pitts, M. K. (1998) Chronic pelvic pain: a meta-analytic review. *Psychology and Health, 13,* 937–951.

McKenna, M. C., Zevon, M. A., Corn, B. & Rounds, J. (1999) Psychological factos and the development of breast cancer: a meta analysis. *Health Psychology,* 18(5), 520–531.

McKinlay, J. B. (1975) Who is really ignorant – Physician or patient? *Journal of Health and Social Behaviour,* 16, 3–11.

McKinstry, B. & Wang, J. (1991) Putting on the style: what patients think of the way their doctor dresses. *British Journal of General Practice,* 41, 275–278.

McLeod, K. S. (2000) Our sense of Snow: the myth of John Snow in medical geography. *Social Science and Medicine, 50*(7–8), 923–935.

McManus, I. C., Winder, B. C. & Gordon, D. (1999) Are UK doctors particularly stressed? *The Lancet,* 354, 1358–1359.

McNaught, A. (1987) *Health Action and Ethnic Minorities.* London: Bedford Square Press.

Meichenbaum, D. (1977) *Cognitive–Behaviour Modification: An integrative approach.* New York: Plenum Press.

Melchart, D., Linde, K., Fischer, P., White, A., Allais, G., Vickers, A. & Berman, B. (1999). Acupuncture for recurrent headaches: a systematic review of randomized controlled trials. *Cephalalgia,* 19(9), 779–786.

Mellanby, A. R., Rees, J. B., & Tripp, J. H. (2000) Peer-led and adult-led school health education: a critical review of available comparative research. *Health Education Research, 15*(5), 533–545.

Melzack, R. (1975) The McGill Pain Questionnaire: major properties and scoring methods. *Pain,* 1, 277–299.

Melzack, R. (1992) Phantom limbs. *Scientific American, April,* 90–96.

Melzack, R. & Wall, P. (1988) *The Challenge of Pain.* London: Penguin.

Melzack, R., Wall, P. D. & Ty, T. C. (1982) Acute pain in an emergency clinic: latency of onset and descriptor patterns. *Pain,* 14, 33–43.

Merskey, H. & Bogduk, N. (1994) *Classification of chronic pain* (210). Seattle, USA: International Association for the Study of Pain Press.

Mestel, R., & Concar, D. (1994) How to heal the body's craving, *New Scientist,* 1st October.

Milgram, S. (1963) Behavioural study of obedience. *Journal of Abnormal and Social Psychology,* 67, 371–378.

Moos, R. H. (1973) Conceptualizations of human environments. *American Psychologist,* 28, 652–665.

Moos, R. H. (1974) *Evaluating Treatment Environments: a social ecological approach.* New York: Wiley.

Moos, R. H. & Moos, B. S. (1981) *Family environment scale manual.* Palo Alto, CA, USA: Consulting Psychologists Press.

Morin, C., Lund, J. P., Clokie, C. M. & Feine, J. S. (2000) Differences between the sexes in post-surgical pain. *Pain,* 2000(85).

Mullen, B. & Johnson, C. (1990) *The Psychology of Consumer Behaviour.* Hove: Lawrence Earlbaum Associates.

Murphy, B., Majella, G. & Oei, T. P. S. (1999) Is there evidence to show Fetal Alcohol Syndrome can be prevented? *Journal of Drug Education,* 29(1), 5–24.

Murphy, L. & Sorenson, S. (1988) Employee behaviours before and after stress management. *Journal of Organisational Behaviour,* 9, 173–182.

Murray, M. & McMillan, C. (1993) Health beliefs, locus of control, emotional control and women's cancer screening behaviour. *British Journal of Clinical Psychology,* 32, 87–100.

Myrtek, M. (2001) Meta-analyses of prospective studies on coronary heart disease, type A personality, and hostility. *International Journal of Cardiology,* 79(2–3), 245–251.

Naldi, L., Peli, L., Parazzini, F. & Carrel, C. F. (2001) Family history of psoriasis, stressful life events, and recent infectious disease are risk factors for a first episode of acute guttate psoriasis: results of a case-control study. *Journal of the American Academy of Dermatology,* 44(3), 433–438.

Natvig, G. K., Albrektsen, G., & Qvarnstrom, U. (2001) Psychosomatic symptoms among victims of school bullying. *Journal of Health Psychology,* 6(4), 365–377.

NHS Executive (1999) *National surveys of NHS patients: General practice 1998*: Department of Health.

Norman, P., Bennett, P., Smith, C. & Murphy, S. (1998) Health locus of control and health behaviour. *Journal of Health Psychology,* 3(2), 171–180.

North Nottinghamshire Health Authority (2001) *Improving the health of young people in North Nottinghamshire*. Mansfield: NNHA.

Office for National Statistics (1998) *General Household Survey for 1996*. London: HMSO.

Office for National Statistics (2000) *Social Trends 30*. London: HMSO.

Ogden, J. (2000) *Health Psychology: a textbook*. (2nd ed.). Buckingham, UK: Open University Press.

Olds, J. & Milner, P. (1954) Positive reinforcement produced by electrical stimulation of the septal area and other regions of the rat brain. *Journal of Comparative and Physiological Psychology,* 47, 419–427.

Orford, J. (1985) *Excessive Appetites: a psychological view of addictions*. Chichester: John Wiley.

Orford, J. (2001) Addiction as excessive appetite. *Addiction,* 96, 15–31.

Orne, M. T. (1962) On the social psychology of the psychological experiment: with particular reference to demand characteristics and their implications. *American Psychologist,* 17, 276–783.

Parks, M. R. & Floyd, K. (1996) Making friends in cyberspace. *Journal of Computer Mediated Communication,* 1(4), Downloaded June 1997 from <http://jmc.huji.ac.il/vol1991/issue1994/parks.html>.

Parrott, A. C. (1998) Nesbitt's Paradox resolved? Stress and arousal modulation during cigarette smoking. *Addiction,* 93(1), 27–39.

Paterson, T., Sullman, M., Kirk, P. & Parker, R. (1998). The impact of regular fluid intake on logging workers. In P. A. Scott, R. S. Bridger & J. Charteris (Eds.), *Global Ergonomics* (pp. 325–328). Oxford: Elsevier.

Pitts, M. (1991a) An Introduction to Health Psychology. In M. Pitts & K. Phillips (Eds.) *The Psychology of Health*. London: Routledge.

Pitts, M. (1991b) The Medical Consultation. In M. Pitts & K. Phillips (Eds.), *The Psychology of Health*. London: Routledge.

Plearce, N. & Quilgares, D. (1996) *Homelessness and ill health*. London: King's Fund.

Plowman, R., Graves, N., Griffin, M., Roberts, J., Swan, A., Cookson, B. & Taylor, L. (2000) *Socio-economic burden of hospital acquired infection*: Central Public Health Laboratory.

Potenza, M. N. (2001) The neurobiology of pathological gambling. *Seminars in Clinical Neuropsychiatry,* 6(3), 217–226.

Power, R., French, R., Connelly, J., George, S., Hawes, D., Hinton, T., Klee, H., Robinson, D., Senior, J., Timms, P. & Warner, D. (1999) Health, health promotion, and homelessness. *British Medical Journal, 318*, 590-592.

Price, D. D., Rafii, A., Watkins, L. R. & Buckingham, B. (1984) A psychophysical analysis of acupuncture analgesia. *Pain,* 19, 27–42.

Prochaska, J. O., DiClemente, C. C. & Norcross, J. C. (1992). In search of how people change: Applications to addictive behaviours. *American Psychologist,* 47, 1102–1114.

Prohaska, T. R., Keller, M. L., Leventhal, E. A. & Leventhal, H. (1987) Impact of symptoms and aging attributions on emotions and coping. *Health Psychology,* 6, 495–514.

Ragland, D. R. & Brand, R. J. (1988) Type A behavior and mortality from coronary heart disease. *New England Journal of Medicine, 318*, 65–70

Ramsey, S. (2001) Audit further exposes UK's worst serial killer. *The Lancet,* 357, 123–124.

Reason, J. (1990) *Human Error*. Cambridge: Cambridge University Press.

Reason, J. (2000) Human error: models and management. *British Medical Journal,* 320, 768–770.

Reyner, L. A. & Horne, J. A. (1998) Evaluation of 'in car' countermeasures to driver sleepiness: cold air and radio. *Sleep,* 21, 46–50.

Richards, J. S., Nepomuceno, C., Riles, M. & Suer, Z. (1982) Assessing pain behaviour: the UAB Pain Behaviour Scale. *Pain,* 14, 393–398.

Riekert, K. & Drotar, D. (1999) Who participates in research on adherence to treatment in insulin-dependent diabetes mellitus? Implications and recommendations for research. *Journal of Pediatric Psychology,* 24(3), 253–258.

Riggio, R. (1990) *Introduction to Industrial/Organisational Psychology*. Illinois, USA: Scott, Foresman and Company.

Ritzer, G. (1993) *The McDonaldization of Society*. CA, USA: Pine Forge.

Robinson, R. & West, R. (1992) A comparison of computer and questionnaire methods of history-taking in a genito-urinary clinic. *Psychology and Health,* 6, 77–84.

Rogers, M. S. & Todd, C. J. (2000) The 'right kind' of pain: Talking about symptoms in outpatient oncology consultation. *Palliative Medicine,* 14(4), 299–307.

Rosenhan, D. L. & Seligman, M. E. P. (1989) *Abnormal Psychology 2nd Ed.* New York: Norton.

Rosenthal, R. & Fode, K. L. (1963) The effect of experimenter bias on the performance of the albino rat. *Behavioural Science,* 8, 183–189.

Roter, D., Lipkin, M. & Korsgaard, A. (1991) Sex differences in patients' and physicians' communication during primary care medical visits. *Medical Care,* 29, 1083–1093.

Roter, D. L. & Hall, J. A. (1992) *Doctors talking with patients/Patients talking with doctors*. Westport, USA: Auburn House.

Rotter, J. B. (1966) Generalised expectancies for internal vs. external control of reinforcement. *Psychological Monographs,* 80(1).

Royal Society for the Prevention of Accidents (2001a) *General accident statistics – January 2001*. London: RoSPA.

Royal Society for the Prevention of Accidents (2001b) *Mobile phones and driving fact sheet*. London: RoSPA.

Rubin, J. (2000) William James and the pathologizing of human experience. *Journal of Humanistic Psychology,* 40(2), 176–226.

Sacker, A., Firth, D., Fitzpatrick, R., Lynch, K. & Bartley, M. (2000) Comparing health inequality in men and women: prospective study of mortality 1986–96. *British Medical Journal,* 320, 1303–1307.

Safer, M. A., Tharps, Q. J., Jackson, T. C. & Leventhal, H. (1979) Determinants of three stages of delay in seeking care at a medical clinic. *Medical Care,* 17, 11–29.

Samet, J. M., Hunt, W. C., Lerchen, M. L. & Goodwin, J. S. (1988) Delay in seeking care for cancer symptoms: A population-based study of elderly New Mexicans. *Journal of the National Cancer Institute,* 80, 432–438.

Sarafino, E. (1994) *Health Psychology: Biopsychosocial Interactions, 2nd Ed.* New York: Wiley.

Saunders, T., Driskell, J. E., Johnston, J. H. & Salas, E. (1996) Journal of Occupational Health Psychology. *1,* 2, 170–86.

Scambler, G. & Scambler, A. (1984) The illness iceberg and aspects of consulting behaviour. In R. Fitzpatrick, J. Hinton, S. Newman & J. Thompson (Eds.), *The Experience of Illness*. London: Tavistock Publications.

Scerri, G. V. & Ratcliffe, R. J. (1994) The goalkeeper's fear of the nets. *Journal of Hand Surgery,* 19(4), 459–460.

Sciacchitano, M., Goldstein, M. B. & DiPlacido, J. (2001) Stress, burnout and hardiness in R.T.s. *Radiology Technology,* 72(4), 321–328.

Selye, H. (1973) The evolution of the stress concept. *American Scientist,* 61, 692–699.

Senior, K. (2001) Should stress carry a health warning? *The Lancet,* 357, 201.

Sherman, J., Hutson, A., Baumstein, S. & Hendeles, L. (2000).Telephoning the patient's pharmacy to assess adherence with asthma medications by measuring refill rate for prescriptions. *Journal of Pediatrics,* 136(4), 532–532.

Shontz, F. C. (1975) *The psychological aspects of physical illness and disability.* New York: Macmillan.

Simpson, T., Murphy, N. & Peck, D. F. (2001) Saliva alcohol concentrations in accident and emergency attendances. *Emergency Medicine Journal,* 18(4), 250–254.

Smedslund, G. (2000) A pragmatic basis for judging models and theories in health psychology: the axiomatic method. *Journal of Health Psychology,* 5(2), 133–149.

Smith, L. A., Oldman, A. D., McQuay, H. J. & Moore, R. A. (2000) Teasing apart quality and validity in systematic reviews: an example from acupuncture trials in chronic neck and back pain. *Pain,* 86, 119–132.

Strax, P. (1978) Evaluation of screening programs for the early diagnosis of breast cancer. *Surgical Clinics of North America,* 58, 667–679.

Streissguth, A. P., Bookstein, F. L., Barr, H. M., Press, S. & Sampson, P. D. (1998) A fetal alcohol behaviour scale. *Alcoholism: Clinical and Experimental Research,* 22(2), 325–333.

Sulik, K. K., Malcolm, C., Webb, J. & Webb, M. A. (1981) Fetal alcohol syndrome (FAS) occurs after one binge drinking episode. *Science,* 214, 936–938.

Sussman, S., Dent, C. W., Simon, T. R., Stacy, A. W., Galaif, E. R., Moss, M. A., Craig, S. & Johnson, C. A. (1995) Immediate impact of social influence-oriented substance abuse prevention curricula in traditional and continuation high schools. *Drugs and Society,* 8, 65–81.

Tannahill, A. (1985). What is health promotion? *Health Education Journal,* 44, 167–168.

Taylor, S. (1986) *Health Psychology.* New York: Random House.

Taylor, S. (1990) Health Psychology; The Science and the Field. *American Psychologist,* 45, 40–50.

Taylor, S. (1999) *Health Psychology.* (4th ed.) New York: McGraw-Hill.

Taylor, S. E., Lichtman, R. R. & Wood, J. V. (1984) Attributions, beliefs about control, and adjustment to breast cancer. *Journal of Personality and Social Psychology,* 46, 489–502.

The Allitt Inquiry (1991) *Independent inquiry relating to deaths and injuries on the children's ward at Grantham and Kesteven General Hospital during the period February to April.* London: HMSO.

Thomas, V. J., Dixon, A. L. & Milligan, P. (1999) Cognitive-behaviour therapy for the management of sickle cell disease pain: an evaluation of a community-based intervention. *British Journal of Health Psychology,* 4(3), 209–229.

Torkington, P. (1991) *Black Health: A political issue.* Liverpool: Catholic Association for Racial Justice.

Townsend, J. (1993) Policies to halve smoking deaths. *Addiction,* 88, 43–52.

Turk, D. C. & Fernandez, E. (1991) Pain: A cognitive–behavioural perspective. In M. Watson (Ed.), *Cancer Patient Care: treatment methods.* Cambridge: BPS Books.

Turner, C., Anderson, P., Fitzpatrick, R., Fowler, G. & Mayon-White, R. (1988) Sexual behaviour, contraceptive practice and knowledge of AIDS of Oxford University students. *Journal of Biosocial Science,* 20, 445–451.

Twisk, J. W., Snel, J., de Vente, W., Kemper, H. C. & van Mechelen, W. (2000) Positive and negative life events: the relationship with coronary heart disease risk factors in young adults. *Journal of Psychosomatic Medicine,* 49(1), 35–42.

Ussher, M. H., Taylor, A. H., West, R. & McEwen, A. (2000) Does exercise aid smoking cessation? A systematic review. *Addiction,* 95(2), 199–208.

van der Spank, J. T., Cambier, D. C., De Paepe, H. M., Danneels, L. A., Witvrouw, E. E. & Beerens, L. (2000) Pain relief in labour by transcutaneous electrical nerve stimulation (TENS). *Archives of Gynecology and Obstetrics,* 264(3), 131–136.

Varni, J. W., Thompson, K. L. & Hanson, V. (1987) The Varni-Thompson Paediatric Pain Questionnaire: I. Chronic musculoskeletal pain in juvenile rheumatoid arthritis. *Pain,* 28, 27–38.

Vomink, J., Matchaba, P. & Garner, P. (2000) Directly observed therapy and treatment adherence. *The Lancet, 355,* 1345–1350.

Wallston, K. A., Wallston, B. S. & Devellis, R. (1978) Development of the multidimensional health locus of control (MHLC) scales. *Health Education Monographs,* 6, 161–170.

Walters, R., Cattan, M., Speller, V. & Stuckleberger, A. (1999) *Proven strategies to improve older people's health.* London: Eurolink Age.

Wardle, J. & Pope, R. (1992) The psychological costs of screening for cancer. *Journal of Psychosomatic Research,* 36, 609–624.

Watson, J. B. (1913) Psychology as the Behaviourist Views it. *Psychological Review,* 20, 158–178.

Weinman, J. (1981) *An Outline of Psychology as Applied to Medicine.* Bristol: John Wright and Sons Ltd.

Weinstein, N. D. (1987) Unrealistic optimism about susceptibility to health problems: Conclusions from a community wide sample. *Journal of Behavioural Medicine,* 10, 481–500.

Weinstein, N. D. (1993) Testing four competing theories of health-protective behaviour. *Health Psychology,* 12, 324–333.

White, P. F., Li, S. & Chiu, J. W. (2001) Electroanalgesia: Its role in acute and chronic pain management. *Anesthesia and Analgesia,* 92(505–13).

Willemsen, G. & Lloyd, C. (2001) The physiology of stressful life experiences. In T. Heller, R. Muston, M. Sidell, & C. Lloyd (Eds.), *Working for Health* (pp. 245–253). London: Sage.

Williamson, J. & Chapin, J. M. (1980) Adverse reactions to prescribed drugs in the elderly: A multicare investigation. *Age and Aging,* 9, 73–80.

Witte, K. & Allen, M. (2000) A meta-analysis of ear appeals: implications for effective public health campaigns. *Health Education and Behavior,* 27(5), 591–615.

Witte, K., Berkowitz, J. M., Cameron, K. & McKeon, J. K. (1998) Preventing the spread of genital warts: using fear appeals to promote self-protective behaviors. *Health Education and Behavior,* 25(5), 571–585.

Wolff, B. B. (1980) Measurement of human pain. In J. J. Bonica (Ed.) *Pain.* New York: Raven Press.

Wolinsky, F. D. & Johnson, R. J. (1991) The use of health services by older adults. *Journal of Gerontology,* 46, S345–S357.

World Health Organisation (1986) *The Ottawa Charter for Health Promotion.* Geneva: World Health Organisation.

Wulfert, E. & Wan, C. K. (1993) Condom use: A self-efficacy model. *Health Psychology,* 12, 346–353.

Zalon, M. L. (1999) Comparison of pain measures in surgical patients. *Journal of Nursing Measurement,* 7(2), 135–152.

Zeigler, S. G., Klinzing, J. & Williamson, K. (1982) The effects of two stress management programs on cardiorespiratory efficiency. *Journal of Sport Psychology,* 4, 280–289.

Zimbardo, P., Ebbesen, E. & Maslach, C. (1977) *Influencing attitudes and changing behaviour, 2nd Ed.* Reading, MA: Addison-Wesley.

Index